Cherishing *your* Wedding

Cherishing *your* Wedding

A Guide to Help Couples Prepare for Marriage in the Catholic Church

KERRY URDZIK

*All books are published thanks
to the generosity of the supporters
of the Catholic Truth Society*

CATHOLIC TRUTH SOCIETY
PUBLISHERS TO THE HOLY SEE

Acknowledgements

Some of the sections of *Cherishing Your Wedding* are inspired by material in the marriage preparation programme *So Great a Mystery*, published by the Diocese of East Anglia.

Nihil Obstat: The Rev. Fr. William Wilson, BSc, BA

Imprimatur: ✠Most Rev. Peter Smith, LLB., J.C. D., K.C.✶H.S., Archbishop of Southwark

Date: 11th January 2018

The *Nihil Obstat* and *Imprimatur* are declarations that a book or pamphlet is free from doctrinal or moral error. No implication is contained therein that those who have granted the *Nihil Obstat* or *Imprimatur* agree with the contents, opinions or statements expressed.

Extracts from scripture are from the New Jerusalem Bible.

Cover image: Wedded couple holding hands. © Ivan Galashchuk/Shutterstock.com

Published 2018 by The Incorporated Catholic Truth Society
40-46 Harleyford Road London SE11 5AY
Tel: 020 7640 0042 Fax: 020 7640 0040
© The Incorporated Catholic Truth Society.

ISBN 978 1 78469 557 6

About the Author

Kerry Urdzik is a life-long Catholic who currently works as the Marriage and Family Life Co-ordinator for the Diocese of East Anglia. She holds a pontifical Bachelor of Divinity degree, and has recently co-authored a new marriage preparation programme which has been implemented for use diocese wide.

In addition to co-ordinating marriage preparation programmes, Kerry supports family life by providing opportunities for marriage and family enrichment, and information for couples on natural fertility awareness. She also gives talks and formation for those interested or working in the area of marriage and family.

Kerry and her husband Chris married in 1988, and they have seven children.

Contents

Introduction 7

Chapter One – Your Engagement: a Time of Preparation 11

Chapter Two – Church Law, Civil Law and Marriage. 20

Chapter Three – Christian Marriage. 28

Chapter Four – Marriage as Sacrament and Covenant 38

Chapter Five – Your Wedding Promises 46

Chapter Six – What Does the Church Say About How and
Where I Get Married? 60

Chapter Seven – Your Wedding Ceremony. 70

Chapter Eight – Your Married Life. 80

Conclusion. 90

Appendices
Family of Origin Reflection Questionnaire 94
Wedding Liturgy Checklist. 96
Suitable Readings for Your Wedding 97
Suitable Music for Your Wedding 99

Introduction

Each of us has an inbuilt desire to love and to be loved. From our earliest days, we thrive on the love showered upon us by our parents and family, and in our friendships we learn kindness, generosity and mutual support. As we approach adulthood, this desire to give love and receive love in return leads many of us to seek an exclusive relationship of total commitment, and while this can be as a priest or religious, for most of us it is as a husband or wife, in marriage. And so somewhere, in the course of going about your business, you met a person that you now know you want to spend the rest of your life with. The better you got to know each other, the more suited you seemed to be. When you imagine your future, he or she features in it. One of you most likely proposed, the other said yes, and now you are both beginning to prepare for the big day. You are about to get married.

Preparation for marriage is a time of great excitement. It is very easy to get swept along on the tide of wedding planning, with its endless lists to make, menus to select, and colour schemes to choose. During this time, it is important not to lose sight of the most important aspect of all: you are preparing for much more than a wedding ceremony, you are preparing to enter into a new stage of your life as a married couple.

Of course, all couples want a beautiful wedding day to remember, and rightly so, although it is important to bear in mind that a wedding does not have to be lavish and expensive to be beautiful – some of the most beautiful weddings are simple and elegant. The elements of wedding planning which do not involve the Church (such as the reception details) will be left to the many and varied publications and *Pinterest* style websites. The purpose of this book is to help support you as you take the time to prepare for marriage, both spiritually and practically (where it relates to your wedding liturgy). Hopefully, you have already taken the time to really get to know each other – marriage should not be a decision made by your heart unless your head is in full agreement! In order to enter into marriage as fruitfully as possible, it is important to take the time to prepare carefully.

Christian marriage is a relationship where two become one

Choosing to marry in the Catholic Church means that there are certain requirements which flow from the Church's understanding of marriage. Catholics are bound to observe these requirements, and we will explore what they are and why this is so. A couple must give adequate notice of their intention to marry to their parish priest in order to give him time to complete the required paperwork and obtain any permissions, but also − most importantly − to give the couple time to prepare for marriage in the Catholic Church. Many countries require six months' notice as a minimum, others as few as three. Regardless of the period of notice required by each Bishops' Conference, it is very important that a couple is adequately prepared for marriage, and it is therefore in their best interests to embark on this as soon as possible. In order to be sure that you are ready and in order to be able to give full consent to marriage, it is important to be clear about what marriage actually *is*.

Christian marriage is a relationship where two become one − "a man leaves his father and mother and is joined to his wife, and the two become one flesh" (*Gn* 2:24). Husband and wife are joined by God, and the baptised are strengthened in their marital union by sacramental grace. The total gift a couple makes of themselves, one to the other, is an icon, or image, of the total self-giving love within the Godhead. The sacrifice and love that each spouse brings to the marriage should draw its strength from the love Christ has for his Church. The fruitfulness of married love is life-giving, both physically as a co-operation with God in the creation of new life, and spiritually, as each spouse is loved, supported and helped to grow in virtue and holiness by the other; and the faithfulness between husband and wife should reflect the complete and total gift of love that God has shown to mankind since the beginning. Marriage, in this sense, can be seen to be a profound reality which points to the communion with God in eternity, the reward to which he calls each one of his children.

We shall explore all these elements further, and see how their meaning is revealed and reflected in the wedding promises you are soon to make. We shall also discuss the various elements of the wedding ceremony itself, both within and outside of Holy Mass, in order to help you plan a liturgy which reflects the profound dignity of Christian marriage in Christ. We will address some common questions and concerns, and each chapter will have suggested practical tips, points for reflection, and prayers. My desire is that, by the end of this book, you will have an increased understanding and appreciation of the marriage into which you are about to enter.

I hope you take time to use this period of engagement to reflect not only upon your relationship with each other, but with God and – importantly – your relationship with God *as a couple*. God wishes to guide you on your journey through life, bless you with his grace and strengthen you when you face difficulties. As children arrive (God willing) and your family grows, you will continue on your journey, stronger now, and influencing those around you as you go. Your family will be one of the building blocks of society, and your witness will be visible for all to see. And all of this from one man and one woman who, in love and faith, and in the presence of God, said "I do..."

How beautiful, then, the marriage of two Christians, two who are one in home, one in desire, one in the way of life they follow, one in the religion they practise... Nothing divides them either in flesh or in spirit... They pray together, they worship together, they fast together; instructing one another, encouraging one another, strengthening one another. Side by side they visit God's church and partake God's banquet, side by side they face difficulties and persecution, share their consolations. They have no secrets from one another; they never shun each other's company; they never bring sorrow to each other's hearts... Seeing this Christ rejoices. To such as these he gives his peace. Where there are two together, there also he is present.

TERTULLIAN

CHAPTER ONE

Your Engagement: a Time of Preparation

Are you ready?

The fact that you picked up this book in the first place indicates that you are probably fairly sure that you are ready for marriage. Occasionally it happens that a couple has not really thought the situation through and is making an impulsive decision. Such a couple may be very smitten with each other and not given much consideration to their future together. But more likely, a couple has indeed thought the matter through very carefully and are as sure as they can be that getting married is the right decision. For these couples, learning more about marriage is not unnecessary – far from it! The more we understand something, the more we tend to appreciate it, and by exploring what marriage is I think you will find a renewed respect for this time honoured institution.

During my time helping couples prepare for marriage, I have found that it can be tricky finding a balanced approach. Some couples may be cautious and perhaps a little reluctant to make a life-long commitment, and for such couples it is important to emphasise the joy which comes from the unbreakable union of husband and wife: you are a team, you have decided you want to make your life journey together, you have both made promises to be faithful, and so you now don't have to worry about the relationship ending the first time you have an epic-sized argument. For others who sometimes make decisions without ample discernment, it is important to emphasise that marriage is for life. We live in times very different from those of our grandparents – where they would save up to purchase something they needed, we tend to rent. Phones are on a payment plan until the next upgrade, cars are very often leased, and even our

True love is the desiring of the genuine good for the other

work contracts tend to be short term; this attitude is beginning to manifest itself in our relationships with others. In his 2014 Address to the World Meeting of Popular Movements, Pope Francis criticised this 'throw away culture' and the abandonment of human relationships when they cease to be valued or productive, a behaviour which both damages the people involved and threatens the very fabric of our society. It is important to stress that marriage is not something we walk away from the moment we are faced with challenges or periods of unhappiness; it is not like a job, where you can look for another position if you find your current employment stressful or unrewarding, nor is it like a vehicle to be traded in when a newer, higher spec model comes along.

For those who are overly cautious, those who are impulsive and those who are somewhere in between, it is important to have a good understanding of marriage as well as realistic expectations. The idea that the most important criteria for a happy marriage are endless romance and finding your 'soul mate' is actually a relatively recent one. It's the disastrous product of a secular society and the Hollywood movie scene. Years ago, people tended to be more pragmatic about marriage, choosing someone who would be a suitable life partner, and with whom they could raise a strong and stable family.

Marriage is truly good and beautiful, but it isn't easy. It will rub the rough edges off both husband and wife, without a doubt. Marriage is the union of two individuals who, even if they have an awful lot in common, will still have a variety of different character traits, preferences and opinions. To top it all off, human beings are prone to selfishness — it's just the way we are, a by-product of Original Sin. Marriage – and parenting – forces us to grow in virtue and to be more patient and generous with others. All relationships involve investing ourselves in others, and love, like friendship, cannot be taken, it can only be received, and it is usually offered in return to that which we give others.

When couples meet and fall in love, there is usually an intense period of attraction. This infatuation phase serves an important purpose in the relationship and is responsible for that powerful and focused interest which drives you to spend a lot of time together and find out all about each other. According to the psychologist Dorothy Tennov, this period lasts no longer than about two years, if that, before settling down. During the period of infatuation, love is blind, as the saying goes, but what should emerge after this is a mature, intentional love.

So what is love, actually? True love, mostly simply put, is the desiring of the genuine good for the other. This is lived out in concrete actions and no longer manifests itself through emotion alone. It moves from a focus on 'how you make me feel' (which is actually quite selfish) to 'what I can do for you' (which is the emergence of self-giving). Life gets busy, we move jobs, move house, and children very often come along, and while it is important to ensure that we never lose sight of the primacy of our marriage over the other demands on our time, it is also well to remember that we are no longer like love-struck teenagers who spend endless hours holding hands and counting the stars. Mature love should realise that although you might sometimes feel neglected when your husband is working late, or if your wife falls asleep nursing the baby, it should never manifest itself by your dwelling on doubts that you married the wrong person or by allowing your eyes and thoughts to contemplate the attractive co-worker at the office.

So, can you look at your future spouse and say: "Yes, I like who you are. I like what you stand for, I respect your views, your interests, your philosophy of life and your dreams. I want you to be the mother/father of our children and the person I share my life with. I know there will be times when life is hard and we are exhausted but I want to commit to sharing all of this with you, and only you."

Are you ready?

Marriage preparation

Preparation for marriage can be broadly divided into the practical and the spiritual, although they overlap and work together to ensure that you are as prepared as you can be for this step you are about to take.

Practical preparation: your relationship and personal circumstances

If you haven't discerned this carefully already, now is the time to be sure you really know each other. People are very complex of course, and you never cease learning about your husband or wife. We are all shaped by our formation and past experiences, and hold opinions based on a set of assumptions. Our perception of our parents' relationship and interactions will have influenced our formation; how they treated each other and their relationship dynamics will have left their impression on us as the way in which the relationship of a married couple works, and it's important to ensure that we are aware of this. If your parents' relationship followed the stereotypical traditional pattern, with your mother doing all the childcare and domestic duties, while your father went out to work and put his feet up in front of the TV in the evenings for example – do you expect your relationship to follow a similar pattern? You may or you may not, that's really not the issue. What matters is that you are aware of it and own it, so to speak, and that you discuss this with your future spouse. Does he or she have the same expectation, or does that scenario horrify them? If so, you may well have some discussion and negotiation to do.

Here's a short story to illustrate another difference which can become apparent in a new marriage. A newly married couple, Emma and Tony, were both from families where their parents were happily married. Emma's parents were quiet by disposition; when tensions arose, very little was said – her mother might sulk for a while until both her parents seemed to have forgotten what the issue was about, and then they carried on about their business. Whether or not the issue was significant, or whether it was resolved (if, in fact, it actually needed to be resolved) was not of concern to Emma, especially while she was young. Nothing disturbed her peace as she went about her play and, later, her school studies. Tony, on the other hand, was from a large Italian family. Their home was nothing if not passionate and loud. There was a great deal of affection in Tony's home, but when tensions arose, everybody knew about it! The arguing was loud, but the storm soon passed. Again, whether the situation was resolved or not escaped the attention of young Tony, who also went about his business as usual.

Emma and Tony brought their childhood experiences to their marriage. While they adored each other, when tensions arose Tony would react in the passionate way he had learned growing up. This was a huge shock to Emma, who was stunned by what she perceived as an unwarranted verbal assault! Her response confused Tony, who thought she was too sensitive. What they both needed was the realisation that while their families of origin were both happy places, they were quite different. They needed to be aware of each other's style of communication, and take steps to modify them where appropriate.

A person's family of origin will have also affected their expectations – if someone has lived through the messy divorce of their parents, they may wonder if it really is possible for a couple to stay together for life. There are many things in our past which will have shaped our future expectations, but the important thing is to be aware of them. Appendix One at the back of this book contains a family of origin reflection exercise. Take some time to complete that and discuss it between the two of you. Understanding where someone is coming from should help you be able to compromise in areas where you disagree. If any of these areas are significant, with you both holding strongly opposing ideas, it may flag a potential future problem. It might be a good idea to seek the advice of someone you trust.

As well as being emotionally prepared for marriage, it is also important that you are financially and practically able to embark on marriage. If you are both living at home, or perhaps are university students, are you able to afford a home of your own or is the plan to move in with one of your parents? If you need the support of your in-laws, have you discussed this with everyone concerned, and do you have a plan with a reasonable timeline? While being affluent is not a prerequisite for marriage, it is important to be able to stand on your own two feet as you begin your lives as a new family. Being newly married always involves a period of adjustment – some couples settle easily into married life, while others may find those first months to be quite rocky. Making sure you are prepared practically for your life together will help minimise any stress in those early days.

And so as soon as you have decided to get married, you will need to contact your parish priest to arrange a meeting. He will talk to you about your particular circumstances. Have either of you been married before? Are you both baptised? All of this will help determine whether he needs to apply for a dispensation of any sort, which we will talk a little more about later. He will ask the Catholic party (or both of you if you are both Catholic) for a recent copy of your Baptism certificate (this copy must be no more than six months old since the sacraments a person receives are annotated in the baptismal register). All of this takes a while, and is part of the reason the Bishops' Conferences of the Church require a minimum period of notice be given to your parish priest.

In addition to sorting out paperwork, your priest will arrange for a programme of marriage preparation. Approaching your priest early not only gives you the best chance of getting the wedding date you prefer, but it is much better to complete your marriage preparation course when you are not rushed or under pressure: too often I see couples preparing for marriage who are distracted by the fact that their wedding is a few short weeks away and they need to double check that the caterer has received their security deposit...

Spiritual preparation

The spiritual part of marriage preparation involves reflection upon marriage – what marriage is, the manner in which it is a path to holiness, and your spiritual life. At the time of the initial meeting with your priest, he will initiate a programme of preparation for getting married in the Catholic Church – this will vary from diocese to diocese, and sometimes from parish to parish. The Church places high priority on good marriage preparation: "so that the 'I do' of the spouses may be a free and responsible act and so that the marriage covenant may have solid and lasting human and Christian foundations, preparation for marriage is of prime importance" (*Catechism of the Catholic Church* (*CCC*) 1632).

Catholic marriage preparation will present opportunities to encourage deeper reflection on Christian marriage as a sacrament, as a covenant, and as a relationship with indispensable elements. As we shall see, it is consent which makes marriage. In order to be able to give our full and free consent on our wedding day, it is important that we understand exactly to what we are consenting. This is not as straightforward as one might think. In today's social climate, we are starting to lose sight of the long-understood meaning of marriage. Many people think that the word marriage can be used to describe a commitment made between two people who love each other and wish to be together in an officially recognised union. Children may or may not be part of this plan. The expected duration of the relationship may vary, with some people deciding that if they fall 'out of love', they will end their marriage and try again. The underlying expectation of many people seems to be that of a lifetime of unlimited, uncomplicated, undying romantic love. Not only is marriage being stripped of much of its meaning, but the expectations that many couples have are, quite simply, unrealistic. Catholic marriage preparation is designed to help couples explore marriage in the Catholic Church, and help them understand the *why* behind the *what* of her teaching.

It is my hope that by preparing as fully as possible for marriage, you will be ready to enter into a strong, happy, life-long union. Life is never certain. People grow and mature, and events unfold. You won't know everything about your future spouse, and if we're all honest about it, we will admit that we don't know everything about ourselves either! Sometimes situations arise that we couldn't have foreseen, and we need to rest assured that we will face them together. This is why we make promises, and these promises are aided by the grace of God.

TO DO

- As a couple, discuss your expectations of what your married life together will be like.

- *Complete the family of origin exercise found in Appendix One.*

- *Ask your priest to give you the blessing for engaged couples as you begin your programme of marriage preparation.*

- *If you are not part of a parish community or regular Sunday Mass goers, consider joining a parish and becoming regular worshippers. Attending the same weekend Mass will enable you to make friends with other like-minded people. They will be a good source of support as you begin your married life.*

REFLECT

Love is never something ready-made, something merely 'given' to man and woman, it is always at the same time a 'task' which they are set. Love should be seen as something which in a sense never 'is' but is always only 'becoming', and what it becomes depends upon the contribution of both persons and the depth of their commitment.

Pope John Paul II, *Love and Responsibility*

PRAY

Prayer is crucial for our faith. It is the lifting of our hearts and minds to God, inviting him into our lives and seeking his help and blessing. If you do not pray daily, this is a good time to start. Pray the 'Three Hail Marys' for purity of mind, heart and body – a beautiful tradition – seeking blessing for your marriage and discernment as you prepare.

Hail Mary, full of grace, the Lord is with thee.
Blessed art thou among women,
and blessed is the fruit of thy womb, Jesus.
Holy Mary, Mother of God, pray for us sinners,
now and at the hour of our death.

AMEN.

CHAPTER TWO

Church Law, Civil Law and Marriage

What is the Church?

Before we look at Church Law, it's worth a short detour to discuss what the Catholic Church *is*. It may not be something you have given much thought to, but it's worth considering especially since we live in a time of unprecedented autonomy. A focus on *my* rights, *my* decisions, even *my* truth is being seen more and more, and a person who is not Catholic may very well ask, "Who is the Church to tell me how to live, anyway?"

I will presuppose a belief in God – in particular in Christianity and the God of Jesus Christ – at this point. There are many people who say they don't believe in God, others who profess a vague notion of the power of the universe, and still others who say they find God in everything. While it is true that God is continually acting to keep his creation in being, Catholics believe in something far more specific than *pantheism*, which is the identification of God with creation or the universe itself. We believe in a loving God who became man in order to suffer, die and rise again *for us*. By taking our sin upon himself, and by being a worthy and effective sacrifice, Jesus restored us to God's friendship after our fall from grace by Original Sin.

Before his passion, death and resurrection, Christ spent three years in what is usually called his public ministry. During this period, he taught his disciples about the kingdom of heaven – how to worship, how to pray, how to live, and how to treat others. And during this period he founded his Church. In a very important passage, we read the following:

When Jesus came to the region of Caesarea Philippi he put this question to his disciples, "Who do people say the Son of man is?" And they said, "Some say John the Baptist, some Elijah, and others Jeremiah or one of the prophets." "But you," he said, "who do you say I am?" Then Simon Peter spoke up and said, "You are the Christ, the Son of the living God." Jesus replied, "Simon son of Jonah, you are a blessed man! Because it was no human agency that revealed this to you but my Father in heaven. So I now say to you: You are Peter and on this rock I will build my community. And the gates of the underworld can never overpower it. I will give you the keys of the kingdom of heaven: whatever you bind on earth will be bound in heaven; whatever you loose on earth will be loosed in heaven."

(Mt 16:13-19)

"You are Peter"

Up until that moment, Peter was known by his given name, Simon. There was no evidence of Peter being used as a name before that time – the word simply meant 'rock'. As with other significant stories in Scripture which chronicle God's unfolding plan of salvation, Jesus changed Simon's name to reflect his new role. This was no random name change, this was a commissioning;

Simon Peter was to be the rock upon which Christ would build his Church. In addition, the meaning behind Jesus's reference to the keys of the kingdom was well known to the Jews – in Isaiah 22, the king's steward carried the keys and along with them, the king's authority. Christ was telling his disciples he would soon be departing, and that he planned to leave his authority with Peter who would hold the keys until his return in glory. The Church therefore recognises Peter as the first pope, and since Christ's authority extends through the ages, on Peter's death it was passed down by apostolic succession. This apostolic succession ensures that the authority given by Christ to Peter still exists in the Church today. Together with Sacred Scripture, the Church looks to Sacred Tradition (the oral tradition of Christ and the apostles handed down through the centuries, especially in her prayers and actions), and the Magisterium to guide the faithful in truth and morals. Consisting of the pope and the world's bishops, the Magisterium is the teaching authority of the Church and serves to safeguard and proclaim the truth of the gospel to subsequent generations, helping us apply this teaching to our lives as the surest path to salvation. The precepts of the Church, for example, such as obligatory Mass attendance on Sundays and holydays, are set by the Church because she knows how easily we could stray from Christ.

The Church is the channel through which Christ continues to guide his people, and through which he dispenses the grace which comes from the merits of his passion, death and resurrection. As a loving mother, the Church has the recipe for human happiness and flourishing, even though there may be times when we, her children, pout and resist her teachings. The Church is the bride of Christ, the people for whom he gave his life, the people he ceaselessly calls to himself. Simply put, it is through Christ and his Church that we have divine life. Through the Church, we receive God's mercy, justice and truth, and it is in the Church that we find the surest path to salvation.

Church Law

Every society needs a system of law in order to function efficiently. The Catholic Church, likewise, has an organisational structure by which she governs herself. This is known as Canon Law, its name deriving from the Greek *kanon* which refers to a measuring rule or standard. Canon Law is a complex system of rules by which the Church abides as she goes about her mission. During the days of the early Church, in books such as the Acts of the Apostles, we see examples of this law developing, for instance the process by which the apostles were replaced (*Ac* 1:15-26), and what to do in the case of various disputes such as whether Gentile converts to Christianity were required to be circumcised (*Ac* 15:1-11). As the Church began to spread and grow, various matters of disagreement were addressed by different popes and councils. Over time, these disputes, and the rulings and decisions which flowed from them, were collated into what was known as Canon Law, now contained in the 1983 *Code of Canon Law* (*CIC*) for the Latin rite Church, which lays out everything the Latin Church needs in order to function.

A baptised Catholic is bound by Church laws in the same way that a citizen is bound by the laws of his or her country. A Catholic who wishes to remain a Catholic 'in good standing' is bound by Canon Law, something which is often referred to as canonical form. It is this canonical form which must be complied with when a Catholic enters into marriage.

The extent to which the Church should be involved in marriage, which is a fundamentally natural institution, was hotly debated at the Council of Trent in the sixteenth century. However, the occurrence of clandestine marriages were resulting in legal disputes, among them challenges to property ownership and the legitimacy of heirs. While the Church is in the business of saving souls rather than solving property disputes, it matters very much whether a marriage is valid in the eyes of God. The only way to ensure this, and to protect all parties involved as well as the institution of marriage itself, was to require that a witness for the Church be present at the wedding. In 1563, the council fathers decreed that "whoever contracts marriage otherwise than in the presence of the pastor and of two or three witnesses, does so invalidly".

Thus, the Church requires that a Catholic entering into marriage must meet the requirements of Church Law. He or she must agree, freely, to promise to abide to what marriage is in front of a bishop, priest or deacon, the usual witness for the Church. There are cases when exceptions can be made, for example the permissibility of being married in a Protestant or Orthodox church, and these will be discussed in Chapter Six.

The laws which deal with marriage are found in canons 1055-1165 of the code. Everything you need to know about Catholic marriage can be found in these chapters, and we will extrapolate the important parts for discussion shortly.

Civil Law

The state is concerned with the legality of marriage, and not with the beliefs and traditions of various religions. In order for the state to recognise marriage, the legal requirements must be complied with. These vary from country to country: even in the UK, there are three different jurisdictions – England and Wales, Scotland, and Northern Ireland. Your parish priest will be familiar with the civil requirements for marriage and let you know what you need to do in this regard. There are several variable elements – in some jurisdictions, priests can be a witness for the state as well as the Church and legally register marriages, while other countries place a degree of separation between the two. Sometimes in the UK a civil registrar will attend the Church wedding, whereas some other countries require two separate ceremonies – one civil, the other religious. This information should be readily accessible from the state agency for registering marriages, and your parish priest will also be able let you know exactly what is required.

The Church, the state and marriage

The Church and the state work together then, to ensure that a couple is legally and validly married in the eyes of both the state and the Church. While both the state and the Church recognise the indispensable role of consent in marriage, the state does not have the same understanding of marriage that the Church has. As a result, there are no requirements for the couple to state anything other than their freedom to marry, and their desire to marry.

The Church, however, thinks very differently. The Church states that marriage is the union of one man and one woman, inseparably joined by God for mutual support and the procreation of children. Marriage should therefore not be closed to the gift of new life, but open to God's blessing of the marital union with children. When preparing to get married, it is important the couple understands the nature of marriage, that it is a life-long union, and not a relationship which exists unless or until one or the other gets disillusioned, at which point they file for divorce and look for someone else. To ensure validity, marriage should be freely and wholeheartedly entered into, without any form of coercion.

Marriage is part of God's plan from the beginning, and will not change based on the prevailing legal, cultural and social trends which either redefine marriage, or allow for easy divorce and subsequent remarriage. This is why the Church requires that a Catholic marry according to the Rite of Matrimony. In the eyes of the Church, a Catholic marrying in a registry office ceremony does not make for a valid marriage; its bare minimum of legal requirements simply will not do.

TO DO

- *Make an appointment to meet with your priest to arrange your wedding date and enrol in a programme of preparation.*

- *Check with the priest to find out the legal requirements of the state if you have not done this already. Make provision to obtain your marriage license and ensure plans are in place to complete required documentation in this area.*

REFLECT

- *Do I believe in the Catholic Church, what she is and her role in my life?*

- *Do I want to be married 'in the Catholic Church', or am I attracted to the tradition of being married in a beautiful church building?*

PRAY

The Apostles' Creed is a summary of the beliefs of the Catholic Church. It is the prayer which we say at the beginning of the Rosary. This is the faith we profess; this is our Catholic faith.

I believe in God,
the Father almighty,
Creator of heaven and earth,
and in Jesus Christ, his only Son, our Lord,
who was conceived by the Holy Spirit,
born of the Virgin Mary,
suffered under Pontius Pilate,
was crucified, died and was buried;
he descended into hell;
on the third day he rose again from the dead;
he ascended into heaven,
and is seated at the right hand of
God the Father almighty;
from there he will come to judge
the living and the dead.
I believe in the Holy Spirit,
the holy catholic Church,
the communion of saints, the forgiveness of sins,
the resurrection of the body,
and life everlasting.

AMEN.

CHAPTER THREE

Christian Marriage

God, the author of marriage

We read in the first book of Sacred Scripture – the book of Genesis – that God called creation into existence. He made the heavens and the earth, the land and the sea and all the creatures of the world. The story is told as the seven days of creation (or, to be precise, six days since God rested on the seventh), and on the sixth day, God created mankind. Up until this point, God had noted that his creation was good, but after the sixth day, in which he created man, he proclaimed his creation "very good". Take a look at the following verses:

> God said, "Let us make man in our own image, in the likeness of ourselves, and let them be masters of the fish of the sea, the birds of heaven, the cattle, all the wild animals and all the creatures that creep along the ground." God created man in the image of himself, in the image of God he created him, male and female he created them. God blessed them, saying to them, "be fruitful, multiply, fill the earth and subdue it. Be masters of the fish of the sea, the birds of heaven and all the living creatures that move on earth." God also said, "Look, to you I give all the seed-bearing plants everywhere on the surface of the earth, and all the trees with seed-bearing fruit; this will be your food. And to all the wild animals, all the birds of heaven and all the living creatures that creep along the ground, I give all the foliage of the plants as their food." And so it was.

> God saw all he had made, and indeed it was very good. Evening came and morning came: the sixth day.

> (Gn 1:26-31)

There is much to be learned from the adjacent verses, but first it is important to re-emphasise that the book of Genesis is not a science manual. The various books of the Bible are comprised of different literary genres, from poetry in the Psalms to historical accounts in the Gospels, and the creation account is not meant to be taken literally in that we need to believe God created the world in six periods of twenty-four hours. What the book does contain, however, is a great and important truth: God is the author of creation and he created mankind as the pinnacle of his work. In the adjacent passage we read that God made man "in our own image, in the likeness of ourselves". Note the allusion to the Holy Trinity here – God in referring to "our image" and not 'my image' is speaking as the Godhead of three persons in communion, Father, Son and Spirit. Male and female together, he made us in his image. God then gave Adam and Eve all of creation to serve them and enable them to be fruitful, to fulfil the earth and subdue it – this is both a blessing *and* a commissioning. God created man and woman for mutual support and companionship – in the second account of creation we read that it was not good for man to be alone; none of the other creatures were like him, none would satisfy his human longings (*Gn* 2:18). From the beginning, then, marriage has existed as a natural vocation – a path to holiness and a way of journeying through life in love and devotion to God and to each other.

And all of this was *very good*.

Marriage after Original Sin

Those of us familiar with the Bible know that this original state of harmony was disrupted very quickly by man's disobedience to God's command, which was to refrain from eating the fruit of the tree of knowledge. God warned that if they did, they would die, and so it came to pass that in doing so – an act which we call Original Sin – we lost the original state of living in harmony with our will and in God's grace. Marriage itself became difficult: it is interesting to note that the very first thing Adam did when God asked him why he had eaten the fruit, was to blame his wife. Moreover, he also blames God! "The woman *you* gave me made me do it" (*Gn* 3:12).

To say it was all a bit of a disaster after Adam and Eve were cast out of paradise would be an understatement. Stories of murder and betrayal, jealousy and unfaithfulness feature strongly in many of the books of Scripture, but God never stopped calling his people back to himself, showing mercy on their suffering. He led them out of slavery in Egypt but asked them to be faithful to him by keeping the law he gave to Moses, which included the Ten Commandments. Despite their promises and good intentions, God's people soon fell again, in one form of disobedience or another, following a pattern which would play out time and again throughout history. The propensity to sin which resulted from the Fall made it hard for people to keep their word, and so by the time of Jesus, divorce was accepted by the Jews. When questioned by the Pharisees about the permissibility of divorce, Jesus gave the following answer:

Then some Pharisees came and tested him by asking, "Is it lawful for a man to divorce his wife for any reason?" Jesus answered, "Have you not read that from the beginning the Creator 'made them male and female' and said, 'For this reason a man will leave his father and mother and be united to his wife, and the two will become one flesh'? So they are no longer two, but one flesh. Therefore what God has joined together, let man not separate."

"Why then," they asked, "did Moses order a man to give his wife a certificate of divorce and send her away?"

Jesus answered, "It was because of your hardness of heart that Moses permitted you to divorce your wives; but it was not this way from the beginning."

(Mt 19:3-8)

In the beginning it was not so, and Jesus calls us back to the beginning by restating the noble goodness of marriage. What God has joined, man cannot separate.

Marriage is used as an image in Sacred Scripture to illustrate the indissoluble bond God has with his people, the theme running like a thread through the different books of the Bible. The Song of Songs is a love story, the prophetic books of Isaiah, Ezekiel and Jeremiah talk of God's nuptial love for his people, and Hosea is a story which tells of adultery and betrayal. Finally, in the last book of the Bible, the Apocalypse (book of Revelation), we read St John's account of his vision of the marriage supper of the Lamb, where Christ is joined in love to us, his people, for all eternity. God's steadfast faithfulness, despite the unfaithfulness of his people, provides the model of fidelity in marriage to which we are called and to which, on our wedding day, we promise.

Marriage in the early Church: the development of doctrine

Two great minds of the Church – St Augustine and St Thomas Aquinas – wrote about Christian marriage, the former in the fifth century and the latter in the thirteenth. They articulated the benefits of marriage in part by discussing the *goods* and the *ends* of marriage, respectively.

St Augustine, bishop of Hippo who died in AD 430, wrote to defend marriage against the heresy of Manichaeism and the utilitarian view of marriage held by the Romans. Manichaeism was the belief that the spirit alone was good and the body and material matters were corrupt, and therefore marriage and the procreation of children were certainly not matters to be celebrated! At the same time, the primary purpose of marriage in Roman society was to protect assets and form alliances which would be of benefit to the state. There was something noble and good about marriage *in itself* that Augustine wished to defend, and he started with the innate human desire for friendship, the highest expression of which, he pointed out, is marriage. In his work *De Bono Conjugali*, Augustine names three goods of marriage: permanence, fidelity and openness to offspring. These three goods are the properties which distinguish marriage from other types of relationship, and are the properties from which marriage takes its glory.

St Thomas Aquinas dealt with marriage is his impressive work the *Summa Theologica*. The primary end of marriage, he wrote, was the procreation of children, while the secondary end was the mutual support of the spouses. He expanded further on these aspects, arguing that the indissolubility of marriage reflected the union of Christ with his Church, and for the absolute necessity of monogamy for the benefit of the children and family.

Marriage in the Lord

And so while Church teaching on marriage has developed through the ages, responding to particular challenges (such as heresy, and the issues surrounding clandestine marriages which we spoke about in the previous chapter), the fundamental truth of marriage remains what it has been "from the beginning":

> *The marriage covenant, by which a man and a woman form with each other an intimate communion of life and love, has been founded and endowed with its own special laws by the Creator. By its very nature it is ordered to the good of the couple, as well as to the generation and education of children. Christ the Lord raised marriage between the baptised to the dignity of a sacrament.*

(CCC 1660)

Marriage in Christian communities rejected polygamy which was practised in many cultures, committing instead to an exclusive union of one man and one woman, together made in the image of God. The Christian understanding of marriage was in fact historically unusual, but became the rule of the West as Christianity evangelised the Roman Empire. Even Roman society, which boasted monogamy, only expected fidelity on the part of the wife; the husband was free to take mistresses and otherwise behave as his mood took him. Christian culture called both husbands and wives to something deeper, exhorting them to love with a Christ-like love. The promises you will make during your Catholic wedding ceremony will reflect this understanding of marriage.

*Four words are
used to describe
marriage – free,
total, faithful
and fruitful*

The essential properties of marriage

Reflecting the Church's understanding of marriage, Canon Law recognises two essential properties which mark marriage, and these are unity and indissolubility. As we will look at later when discussing marriage as a sacrament, what something *is* can be different from what it looks like. The Eucharist is an example of this – it is truly the presence of Jesus, but under the appearance of bread and wine. Likewise, in marriage there is a total union of husband and wife, joined by an unbreakable bond, and while it may be hard to visualise this bond since you both look remarkably the same as you did before your wedding, the reality remains that a married couple is a distinct reality, something more than the sum of its parts.

There are four words which are also often used to describe marriage – free, total, faithful and fruitful. Firstly – and most importantly – marriage must be entered into freely. The indispensable element of marriage is the consent of bride and groom; Canon Law states that "the consent of the parties, legitimately manifested between persons qualified by law, makes marriage; no human power is able to supply this consent" (*CIC* 1057.1). Only the bride and groom can give this consent – nobody can give it on their behalf. Are you familiar with the words "who gives this woman to be married to this man"? It's an antiquated tradition, stemming from the time when a woman was considered the father's property until given to her husband. You will never hear these words in a Catholic marriage, however; the bride's freedom is so important that nothing should call this into question. It is actually preferred that the bride and groom walk down the aisle together, since this is a visual sign that the two are freely choosing marriage, but the tradition of a father walking his daughter down the aisle is very moving to watch and it remains commonplace. A father (or another relative) escorting the bride on her wedding day is a perfectly acceptable custom.

Secondly, marriage must be total. The total gift of spouses, one to the other, manifests itself physically and spiritually. It incorporates the next two aspects – faithfulness and fruitfulness. A total gift of self will not be unfaithful in thought, word or deed. This total gift is irrevocable, involving a promise to love until death, and this is part of the promise we make on our wedding day. A promise of total fidelity gives no room for us to entertain the thought that we will get divorced if things don't work out.

Similarly, the total gift of self must be open to new life, to the gift of children. It is a beautiful thing to contemplate that the invisible love of a husband and wife can manifest itself physically as a new and distinct human being. Being open to life does not mean that children will always arrive, and it is important to distinguish between a refusal to have children and the inability to have children. Couples who bear the cross of infertility, or those who marry in later life after their childbearing years have passed are not deliberately frustrating God's plan. Their situation is not the result of a deliberate act on their part to exclude children. It is important to note – perhaps especially in instances such as these – that marriage is not only physically fruitful, but also spiritually fruitful. Together, a husband and wife help each other grow in holiness; living with another who loves us unconditionally, and who will be honest with us can help us thrive and grow in virtue. Like hiking on a rugged path while holding each other's hand over the rocky sections, your spouse can give you encouragement on days when you are doubtful and you likewise, can help them when times get tough for them. You are in this together, and the mutual support, love and respect you give to each other is a joy to behold.

The faithfulness which we discussed in practical terms in the previous chapter has its roots in the understanding of marriage as a reflection of the relationship of Christ with his Church. Christ established a new covenant – Christ is the head and we are the body (*Col* 1:18); he is the vine and we are the branches (*Jn* 15:5). The inseparable nature of Christ with us, his people, is reflected in the inseparability of husband and wife. This union is sacred and our spouse should be our priority, to love, comfort and protect, forsaking all others. We will now look at these elements of marriage closely as they are addressed in the wedding promises you are about to make.

TO DO

- *Discuss with your future spouse the different aspects of marriage.*

- *Discuss with your future spouse the expectations you have about work and children.*

REFLECT

Marriage is more than your love for each other. It has a higher dignity and power, for it is God's holy ordinance, through which he wills to perpetuate the human race till the end of time. In your love you see only your two selves in the world, but in marriage you are a link in the chain of the generations, which God causes to come and to pass away to his glory, and calls into his kingdom. In your love, you see only the heaven of your own happiness, but in marriage you are placed at a post of responsibility towards the world and mankind. Your love is your own private possession, but marriage is more than something personal – it is a status, an office.

Just as it is the crown, and not merely the will to rule, that makes the king, so it is marriage, and not merely your love for each other, that joins you together in the sight of God and man.

Dietrich Bonhoeffer

PRAY

O most Sacred Heart of Jesus, King and centre
of all hearts, dwell in our hearts and be our
King; grant us by Your grace to love each other
truly and chastely, even as You have loved Your
spotless Bride, the Church, and have given
Yourself up for her.

Bestow upon us that mutual love and Christian
forbearance which are so highly acceptable in
your sight, and a mutual patience in bearing
each other's defects; for we are certain that
no living creature is free from them. Do not
permit even the slightest defect to mar that full
and gentle harmony of spirit, the foundation of
the mutual assistance in the many and varied
hardships of life, that is the end for which
woman was created and united inseparably to
her husband.

FRANCIS L FILAS, SJ

CHAPTER FOUR

Marriage as Sacrament and Covenant

Sacramental theology revisited

You may remember from your childhood catechism classes that there are seven sacraments: Baptism, Confirmation, the Eucharist (also known as Holy Communion), Penance (Confession), the Anointing of the Sick, Holy Orders and Matrimony. St Augustine in the fifth century provided a nice, tidy definition – a sacrament is "an outward and visible sign of an inward and invisible grace".

Grace is God's life in us. One of the consequences of Original Sin (which we read about in the book of Genesis) was that by eating the fruit of the tree – that is, by disobeying God's command – we would die (Gn 2:17). Pain and suffering entered the world, and the loss of God's grace left us dead in our sin. Following our redemption through the suffering, death and resurrection of Christ, God's grace has been made available to us once more. Actual grace comes to us at different times, through impulses to take a certain kind of action for example, and always reflects God's care for us. Actual grace differs from sacramental grace, however, in that the latter abides in the soul and effects a real change in us. We receive sacramental grace initially on the occasion of our Baptism, but also on other particular occasions in our life.

We can see in each sacrament the visible sign: the water poured at Baptism, the oil at Confirmation, the bread and wine which become the real presence of Christ in the Eucharist, the words spoken in Confession. These "outward signs" are easy to spot, but what is actually going on is the invisible outpouring of the grace of God into our souls. This is a very profound reality, although hard to understand. And so too, in marriage between a baptised couple, God bestows his sanctifying grace.

The sacrament of marriage

In the sacrament of marriage, it is the words spoken by the bride and groom which are the physical signs of the sacrament. Unlike the other sacraments which are ordinarily ministered by a member of the clergy, in the case of Matrimony in the Latin Rite Catholic Church, it is not the priest who confers the sacrament on the couple but the baptised couple who confer the sacrament on each other. God pours forth his grace, blessing and strengthening the marriage which has just been entered into by husband and wife. The sacramental grace of Matrimony perfects the natural love of husband and wife, raising their love to a supernatural level which surpasses the couple's natural affection for each other. It blesses the marital union, so that together the couple grows in holiness – marriage is a vocation which is a path to heaven. The grace of the sacrament helps the couple make prudent decisions, aids them in raising their children, and enables them to deal with each other's shortcomings.

A marriage between two baptised Christians is always a sacrament, whether or not they know it or intend it: Canon Law states that "the matrimonial covenant, by which a man and a woman establish between themselves a partnership of the whole of life and which is ordered by its nature to the good of the spouses and the procreation and education of offspring, has been raised by Christ the Lord to the dignity of a sacrament between the baptised. For this reason, a valid matrimonial contract cannot exist between the baptised without it being by that fact a sacrament" (*CIC* 1055).

Marriage as covenant

It is also very important to understand that marriage is so much more than a contract. In the case of a contract, the parties are bound by certain terms and conditions. If one party does not uphold their end, he or she is in violation of the contract, and it can be dissolved. Marriage is not like this, however. Husband and wife do not marry contingent upon particular terms and conditions: if I go out to work, you will make my dinner when I come home, or, if we have children, I will change the nappies and you can do the bathing. While tensions surely can and do arise when one, or both spouses feel overworked and under-supported, this is not grounds for divorce precisely because marriage is *not* a simple contractual agreement.

Marriage, rather, is a covenantal relationship. A covenant binds two people together; in ancient cultures, covenants were entered into by individuals or tribes to help ensure protection and prosperity. They were never entered into lightly, instead always requiring solemn promises which were witnessed before God, very often involving blood exchange or animal sacrifice. In the Old Testament we see a continuation of this practice, only now we see the emergence of God making covenants with mankind. This is quite remarkable if you think about it: the inequality in status between God and us – his creatures – makes it seem absurd that he would bind himself to us in an unbreakable union, but that's exactly what he did. First with a couple, Adam and Eve, then with a family (illustrated by the promise he gave to Noah to never flood the earth again), third with a tribe led by Abraham, followed by one with a nation (the law given to Moses in the Exodus), and then with a kingdom with David, to whom the Messiah was promised. In all of these covenants, God remained faithful, but his people did not. Time after time, mankind broke the promises they had intended to keep, but God did not abandon his people. In the fullness of time, God became man in the Incarnation, in the person of Jesus of Nazareth, the Christ. Jesus established a new covenant with all of us, calling us into a familial relationship, and we should never underestimate the immense significance of God – the author of all existence – calling human beings into a relationship where we are made his family.

The marital union of husband and wife is likewise the joining of persons and the creation of a family unit. This covenant, true to form, is a solemn declaration before God and man to love and to cherish, no matter what the future holds. None of us knows what that might be – in all likelihood, there will be many times of great joy. But there may also be times of stress and unemployment, times of sickness. What if you found out you were having triplets? Very joyful, yes; easy, I would venture probably not! This promise to love 'no matter what' is a reflection of the total love and fidelity God has for us.

It should be a thing of joy, then, that your marriage will be a covenant and not a simple contract. You don't have to worry that your wife will leave you if you say the wrong thing, or that your husband will walk off with another woman who is a little younger and maybe a bit prettier than you as the years go by. In this confidence, we are free to grow and flourish, and raise our families secure in the knowledge that we are a team... no matter what.

Do you see now why the Church says that a valid marriage is an indissoluble union? Yes, the two of you still go about your daily business as two individuals, but in reality, you are part of a union, *made one in the flesh*. Since something that is truly one cannot be torn apart, a marriage of husband and wife, whom God has joined, must not be separated by man.

The wedding liturgy: a celebration of the whole Church

The sacrament of Matrimony takes place within the wedding liturgy. Since the Church is the body of Christ, we are bound to one another as Christians by virtue of our Baptism. The liturgy is a public act of worship, rich in symbolism, one which follows a particular structure. It is a celebration of the whole Church, and this remains true even though people may be gathered to celebrate a particular event such as the Baptism of a child, or the wedding of a couple in love. With every sacrament, the whole Church is strengthened. It is partly for this reason that the wedding liturgy follows a particular set of norms – the hymns, the readings, the wedding promises – all of these reflect the solemnity of marriage as a celebration of the whole Church and an act of worship offered to God.

Three to get married

Three to Get Married is the name of a very good book by Fulton J Sheen. Behind this title is the idea that there are three in a marriage – husband, wife and God. Left to our own devices, love tends to be self-seeking. We are often in love with the idea of love, that it will be endlessly rewarding and pleasurable. When the shine wears off, we can become disillusioned. One measure by which we often judge the success of our marriage is that of the sexual relationship.

In our society today, we seem overly focused on sex. The sexual expression of love is a very beautiful thing within marriage, where it illustrates the total self-gift between spouses. The Church recognises and celebrates this

God-given gift, yet to place too much emphasis on this physical intimacy, or see it as the primary measure of love, is a mistake. When the passion starts to fade, a couple may think their love, too, is fading. The Church is not puritanical about sex, seeing it as something distasteful or something to be avoided, but she cautions against its misuse precisely because it is so powerful and beautiful. For this reason it belongs only within marriage, and it should always be approached with a sacred reverence.

Placing God at the centre of our marriage ensures that love grows authentically. As a couple grows in faith and virtue, husband and wife are able to genuinely love and support each other. Looking to the Gospel as a guide for Christian living, and focusing on the cross as the example of perfect love, a couple living their faith together can realise this intimate union, growing closer to each other the closer they draw to God. This is illustrated in the image below:

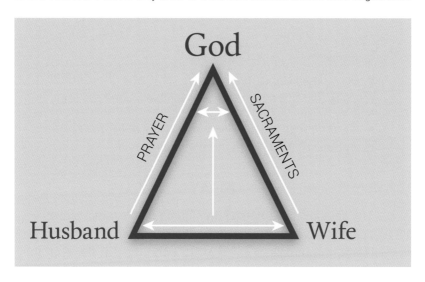

We grow in faith with the help of prayer and the sacraments. Our selfishness is tempered, our priorities reordered perhaps, as we become more aware of the important things in life. This relationship of three – husband, wife and God – will form the firmest foundation for a marriage and for raising children if and when they arrive. As the author of the book of Ecclesiastes writes, "A threefold cord is not quickly broken" (Qo 4:12).

TO DO

- *Pray every day! This seems simple and straightforward, but we cannot hope to know and love God if we spend very little time in his presence. Similarly, discerning his will for our lives – which will ultimately bring us personal fulfilment – is much harder without spending time in prayer each day. It doesn't have to be a lot of time. You can speak to him simply, read some Scripture, or recite one of the prayers of the Church – a combination of all three is ideal.*

REFLECT

- *Do I understand more clearly now why the Church teaches that marriage is an indissoluble union?*

- *If I'm honest, what is the state of my faith? Do I pray every day? Should I learn more about my faith?*

PRAY

The Angelus is a prayer of the Church that is traditionally prayed three times a day – at the beginning of the day (6am), the middle of the day (12 noon) and at the end of the day (6pm). In some countries such as Ireland, the Angelus Bells are rung at noon to remind those working in the fields to stop and pray. The Angelus, as the name implies, gets its name from the Angelic Salutation – the angel Gabriel greeting Mary with the news she would give birth to the Son of God. The story of our salvation begins...

The Angel of the Lord declared unto Mary:
And she conceived of the Holy Spirit.

*Hail Mary, full of grace, the Lord is with thee;
blessed art thou among women and blessed is
the fruit of thy womb, Jesus. Holy Mary, Mother
of God, pray for us sinners, now and at the hour
of our death. Amen.*

Behold the handmaid of the Lord:
Be it done unto me according to thy word.

Hail Mary...

And the Word was made flesh:
And dwelt among us.

Hail Mary...

Pray for us, O Holy Mother of God.
*That we may be made worthy of the promises
of Christ.*

Let us pray:
Pour forth, we beseech thee, O Lord,
thy grace into our hearts; that we,
to whom the Incarnation of Christ, thy Son,
was made known by the message of an angel,
may by his passion and cross be brought
to the glory of his resurrection,
through the same Christ Our Lord.

AMEN.

CHAPTER FIVE

Your Wedding Promises

In this chapter, we will look at the questions asked by the priest before consent and the wedding promises declared by the bride and groom. All of the words spoken are important and indispensable; they reflect that the bride and groom are giving their free and full consent to marriage, which is a union in which they promise to be faithful to each other as long as they live, and in which they will be open to the gift of new life. Let's explore these elements and some things which may affect them.

Establishing consent

The bishop, priest or deacon officiating your wedding will ask you both a question to establish your consent. Different countries may use different translations of the Rite of Marriage, but even if the words are subtly different, the question remains fundamentally the same. In England and Wales the words are thus:

"N and N, have you come here to enter into marriage without coercion, freely and wholeheartedly?"

Since "consent makes marriage" (*CCC* 1626), it is crucially important that the bishop, priest or deacon who receives your consent for the Church is in no doubt of your free and full consent.

There are many factors which can affect freedom of consent. An easy example to spot would be the shotgun wedding, a caricature of times past, where a father forces the groom to marry his daughter (who is very often expecting a baby) at gunpoint. While these days in Western cultures we see nothing quite that dramatic, there are still cases where couples may feel forced by circumstances into marriage. A couple who are faced with an unexpected pregnancy may decide they need to 'do the right thing' and get married even

though they may not have been considering marriage at all until they saw those lines on the positive pregnancy test. The Church can sometimes be reluctant to marry a couple who come citing this as the reason for their wedding, since if the marriage falls apart down the road, this lack of full and free consent can call the validity of the marriage into question.

A difficult family situation can also affect freedom of consent. A bride who was starting to have second thoughts about her fiancé when she discovered her mother had terminal cancer and not long to live, for example, would likely find herself in a difficult position. If the mother was very fond of her future son-in-law, and longed for nothing more than to see them married before her death, it would be very difficult for the bride to call off the wedding. She may sweep her doubts under the carpet and proceed as planned.

Sometimes things that affect freedom are not as clearly defined and easy to identify as unplanned pregnancies or family crises. Sometimes they unfold gradually. A couple may move in together – something which has become very commonplace in our time. If the relationship starts to show some cracks, they may decide to get married to see if that makes a difference. After all, they have a mortgage and a dog and it would be too hard to sort out a separation...

Cohabiting couples in a situation such as this should ask themselves: regarding our marriage – are we sliding, or deciding?

To what are we consenting, exactly?

In order to freely consent to marriage, it is important to know what marriage *is*. If we consent to what we *think* marriage is (for example, a romantic union in which we plan to find personal fulfilment at all times) and then walk away if and when we are disappointed, we have not intended to love each other 'for better, for worse'. The wedding promises are there to reflect this indissoluble union – we promise to stay for the long term, even if we find it difficult at times. And so the Church needs to ascertain that a couple understands this and is prepared to make this promise. (Again, each jurisdiction may have slightly different wording, but this important aspect of marriage will always be ascertained.) In England and Wales, the question asked by the priest is:

> *N, are you resolved to take N to be your wife: to love her, comfort her, honour and protect her, and forsaking all others, to be faithful to her as long as you both shall live?*

> *N, are you resolved to take N to be your husband: to love him, comfort him, honour and protect him, and forsaking all others, to be faithful to him as long as you both shall live?*

Married love is a beautiful thing, and while the initial flush of romantic infatuation will pass, it will develop into a solid, secure love which reflects a deep care and consideration for the wellbeing of your spouse. This mutual good of the spouses brings joy throughout the years, but it will require a degree of maturity to negotiate challenges and times of difficulty. The bride and groom must each ask themselves: am I prepared to promise to love and support my spouse from now forward, to the very best of my ability?

Likewise, are the bride and groom prepared to promise to be faithful to each other, until death? Married love in being faithful requires exclusivity. Adultery has always been a grave matter and can shatter a marriage and destroy trust; the pain of betrayal is very deep. Faithfulness, however, goes beyond our actions, it is an attitude. Jesus tells his disciples, "You have heard that it was said, 'You shall not commit adultery.' But I tell you that anyone who looks at a woman lustfully has already committed adultery with her in his heart" (*Mt* 5:27-28).

On first impression, that can seem a bit extreme; after all, who doesn't notice an especially attractive woman or man when they are out and about? Yet Jesus is not talking about simply noticing another person; in using the word 'lust' he is referring to entertaining and dwelling on thoughts of an improper nature. This attitude is unfaithful since it involves entertaining thoughts of a sexual kind about someone who isn't our spouse; moreover, if we had opportunity to act upon these thoughts, could we be sure we wouldn't?

Married love in being faithful requires exclusivity

Also worthy of mention is the topic of pornography and its widespread use in our society today. Pornography is hugely dehumanising for both women and men. Numerous studies reflect its damage to relationships, and pornography is cited as a major contributing factor in more than 50% of divorces. It contributes to unrealistic expectations about sexuality, and exploits and degrades everybody involved in its production and consumption; when pornography comes into our homes, it completely destroys marital intimacy between husband and wife. Our love and attention belong to our spouse alone; spending time looking at and fantasising about other people turns sexual activity into an inwardly focused, self-gratifying act instead of a loving gift of ourselves to our spouse. This is 'committing adultery in our heart', no matter how someone may attempt to justify it as harmless. In addition, it is possible that porn addiction can affect marital consent, since it can skew a person's perspective of reality to such an extent that they are either unable to see the reality of the married state, or are unable to assume the obligations expected of them. All of that being said, it is important for someone who struggles in this area not to feel despondent or defeated. The sacrament of Confession is a confidential place to discuss this matter if necessary – it is a very common problem which priests hear about frequently, and the grace of the sacrament can help overcome any compulsion which exists. There are also many online resources designed to help people who realise that pornography is destructive but aren't able to stop viewing it, such as *Porn No More* and *Integrity Restored*. Free internet accountability software such as *X3Watch* can help too.

Openness to life

The third question posed to bride and groom directly addresses their willingness to accept children:

"Are you prepared to accept children lovingly from God and to bring them up according to the law of Christ and his Church?"

Are we giving our consent to be co-creators of new life with God, to allow him to act in our lives and bring new members of the Christian family into existence? If, at the time of their wedding, a couple has made up their mind that they will not have any children, they have excluded one of the goods, or ends, of marriage. Making such a decision would render their marriage invalid. In addition, placing conditions upon the procreative aspect of marriage (for example, a mentality which says there will only be children *if and when I decide to try for them*), or that the marriage is contingent upon the birth of future children, would similarly affect the validity of the marriage.

By asking husband and wife to be open to life, we are directed back to the commissioning of Adam and Eve – to be fruitful and multiply. We are called to procreate with God, procreation being substantially different from reproduction. Both human beings and animals have the genetic material within them to enable reproduction, but only God creates the soul. Human beings, being both body and immortal soul, co-operate with God to bring new life into the world and build up God's kingdom.

Marriage manifests its physical fruitfulness, then, by the procreation of children which are usually born into a marriage. The Church teaches that children are the crowning glory of marriage (*CCC* 1652), and watching your family grow brings a lot of joy and gladness. Of course, children are very demanding and nothing cures us of our selfishness more than being forced to get out of bed in the middle of the night and put the demands of another person before our own. Children contribute to our sanctity and help us grow in virtue; they make us better people! It is important to talk this aspect of marriage over with your future spouse; many couples enter into marriage without discussing their thoughts about children and how they will be raised, often making assumptions that later become a cause for disagreement and anxiety.

There will be some couples who are unable to have children, and this brings a unique type of suffering. Infertility can be a tremendously heavy cross to bear, and requires a long period of readjustment to the circumstances. We are all called to spiritual parenthood and fruitfulness, by way of supporting other families or the adoption or fostering of children.

Sexual morality: Theology of the Body and planning your family

The Church holds sexuality to be worthy of reverence and respect, since it is the most profound way of expressing a deep intimacy between husband and wife. Pope St John Paul II gave a series of Wednesday Audiences between 1979 and 1984 which were later compiled and known collectively as *The Theology of the Body*. While very beautiful and thorough, this work in its original form is lengthy; some good summaries have been produced which make his work much more accessible. Pope St John Paul II's fundamental point for our purpose in preparing for marriage is that it is through our body we express ourselves, and it is through our body that we can come to learn about God.

Our body speaks a language. From a simple hug or handshake, to sexual intercourse, what we do with our body conveys meaning. Sexual intercourse is the language of total and exclusive self-giving, our actions saying, "I give myself totally to you, all that I am and all that I have". If we withhold our fertility, seeking the sexual pleasure in isolation from a complete and total gift of ourselves, the integrity of the marriage act is destroyed.

This divorce of the unitive from the procreative meaning of sexual intercourse is behind the Church's teaching that contraception is always impermissible. In 1968, Pope Paul VI issued an encyclical — *Humanae Vitae* — which explains the Church's understanding of sexuality, together with what

turned out to be a prophetic vision of what a contraceptive society would look like. It is not a difficult read, and worth a look if you are struggling with this particular teaching.

The Church's teaching in the area of sexual morality is very countercultural, and one which can meet with a lot of resistance. Couples are, understandably, apprehensive about having baby after baby until the wife feels like the *Old Woman Who Lived in a Shoe*, but the Church teaches that natural fertility awareness methods are permissible in marriage; in fact, she is fully supportive of responsible parenthood by encouraging the couple to discern the spacing of children in response to many different factors which affect their family – emotional, physical and financial.

Fertility awareness methods rely on external observable signs which accurately reflect the internal stage of the woman's reproductive cycle. It is important to learn from a qualified teacher, but fundamentally, it works as follows: the hormone oestrogen is produced, preparing the egg for release, and the cervical mucus which is produced in response to this hormone aids sperm motility. It is the presence of this mucus which indicates fertility. Once the egg is released, progesterone is produced causing an upward temperature shift and the drying up of mucus. The woman ceases to be fertile following the observation of these signs. If your cycle is 23 days one month and 45 the next, these signs remain the same enabling the methods to be used with complete confidence; likewise with breastfeeding mothers and peri-menopausal women. Fertility awareness methods, which include Billings, Sympto-Thermal and Creighton, are as reliable as the contraceptive pill. (A quick Google search will give you contact information of teachers of the various methods if you wish to learn.) A couple can interpret these external signs, and time intercourse in order to achieve or avoid pregnancy. There are no side effects; however it does require a couple to abstain from sexual intercourse for a few days during the fertile period. This can be challenging, but has many positive effects: it encourages an appreciation of fertility, improved communication, the nurturing of other ways of showing affection, growth in the virtue of self-control, and generosity – things that make for a happy marriage generally. It may well be for these reasons that couples using natural family planning have a 2-4% divorce rate, while Catholics who are using contraception have a divorce rate which mirrors the rest of society (in the UK, around 42% in 2013).

Natural family planning is *not* the same as contraception. Even if you choose to avoid pregnancy by abstaining from sex during the fertile time, you are not destroying the integrity of the marital act which remains, each time, a total gift of self. Contraception renders marital intimacy a partial gift of self,

Children are a gift from God, a blessing which he bestows

and closed off to the gift of new life. The sexual union of husband and wife is a profoundly powerful expression of marital love, and contraception excludes its God-given creative potential. I remember hearing the Catholic philosopher and theologian Alice von Hildebrand speak. She said that, regarding the Church's teaching on contraception, people often say that they don't want the pope in their bedroom. "Neither do I want the pope in my bedroom!" she replied. "But I do want the Holy Spirit there!"

Lastly, a brief word about the Church's teaching on In Vitro Fertilisation. Children are a gift from God, a blessing which he bestows on husband and wife. There will be some couples, though, who are unable to conceive. First of all, it would be worthwhile learning the Creighton method of fertility awareness, since this can sometimes flag up problems with fertility which can be corrected, enabling the couple to go on and conceive naturally. But if this is not possible, the Church teaches that IVF is not permitted because it separates the unitive and procreative aspects of lovemaking. In addition, many embryos are created, more than are usually implanted, and this often results in their destruction. IVF is harmful to the dignity due to all human life, and in a sense it contributes to viewing a child as something one can acquire by any means possible rather than a blessing from God. This can be a very hard teaching to take for a couple bearing the cross of infertility. The Church is not dismissive of an infertile couple's pain, but she must proclaim the truth of the meaning of the sexual act and the value of all human life from conception till natural death.

Parent as first educator

The *bonum prolis* – the good of children – as mentioned by St Augustine and discussed in Chapter Three includes the rearing and education of children. Having children is just the first step. God places on us the responsibility to raise our children (*his* children) in the faith by leading them in prayer, bringing them to Mass and teaching them about who he is. The Church takes this responsibility very seriously, so seriously, in fact, that in the case of a mixed marriage (that is, either the bride or groom is not Catholic), the Catholic party must sign the following statement:

> *I declare that I am ready to uphold my Catholic faith and avoid all dangers of falling away from it. Moreover, I sincerely undertake that I will do all that I can within the unity of our partnership to have all the children of our marriage baptised and brought up in the Catholic Church.*

In promising to raise our children in the Church, we are accepting the responsibility (and claiming our right) as the primary educator of our children. While most of us choose to send our children to school when they are of school age (instead of educating them at home), the school acts with our authority. We have the *right* to teach our children in the context of our morals and a *duty* to do so, and this involves protecting them from material which undermines their innocence or their faith. A huge amount of information is learned by our

child before they reach school age – language and appropriate social skills, motor skills such as walking and dressing, good manners – all of these are taught by us, their parents. We must be confident in our ability to guide our children through life, especially in the early years.

When it comes to raising children in the Catholic faith, some argue that that children should be free to choose their faith for themselves when they are older. However, if we believe something is genuinely important and good for our child, we do not let them choose for themselves! This is true of healthy eating, tooth brushing and education, to name but a few. We know that a lack of tooth brushing leads to tooth loss, and we firmly believe that a good set of teeth is important. If we make sure our children clean their teeth when young, we have done what is required of us; if they choose to throw out their toothbrush when they turn eighteen, then that's their decision. I propose that the same is true of our faith. If we firmly believe that we are made for God and he is our eternal destiny, this faith formation is too important to neglect in our child's formative years.

Words of consent

Following the question about a couple's preparedness to accept children, the bishop, priest or deacon will receive the consent of the couple on behalf of the Catholic Church. He will ask you to repeat words the same as, or similar to, the following:

I call upon these persons here present to witness that I, N, do take thee, N, to be my lawful wedded wife, to have and to hold from this day forward for better, for worse, for richer, for poorer, in sickness and in health, to love and to cherish till death do us part.

I call upon these persons here present to witness that I, N, do take thee, N, to be my lawful wedded husband, to have and to hold from this day forward for better, for worse, for richer, for poorer, in sickness and in health, to love and to cherish till death do us part.

The words spoken here must also be unconditional. We mentioned the mindset which can affect a couple's attitude towards children earlier in this chapter, but this also extends to other aspects of life. We cannot promise to stay married 'as long as' my spouse is financially successful or physically healthy; the gift we make of ourselves on our wedding day must be an unconditional, total gift.

These words of consent are powerful and beautiful — take some time to reflect upon them as you prepare for your wedding. If you're like I was, you will have a million things on your mind, from wondering if your guests will have enough to eat at the reception, to whether the weather might spoil the pictures. Take a breath, step back and look at the words above. You are about to begin a new stage in your life, as part of a married couple. What you are about to do will be blessed by God, and it is truly good.

TO DO

- *Discuss the Church's teaching on contraception and natural family planning with your fiancé(e).*

REFLECT

Every threat to the family is a threat to society itself. The future of humanity, as St John Paul II often said, passes through the family. The future passes through the family. So protect your families! Protect your families! See in them your country's greatest treasure and nourish them always by prayer and the grace of the sacraments.

Pope Francis, Address to Families,
Manilla, Philippines, 16th January 2015

PRAY

Louis and Zelié Martin were the parents of St Thérèse of Lisieux, sometimes called the Little Flower. Examples of a married couple who lived a life of heroic virtue, they were canonised together on 18th October 2015. Their feast day is 12th July.

Saints Louis and Zelié Martin, after having had the desire for religious life, you heard the Lord's call to the vocation of marriage.

You are the "parents without equal" of whom your daughter St Thérèse of the Child Jesus speaks; the fortunate parents of Léonie, the Servant of God, Sister Françoise-Thérèse; of Marie, Pauline, and Céline, transplanted to Mount Carmel; and of the four children taken from your affection in their youth: Hélène, Joseph, Jean-Baptiste, and Mélanie-Thérèse.

You gave all glory to God through your humble and patient work, your commitment to the poor, and your family life, where reigned the happiness of loving and being loved.

You lived your daily life concretely through the joys and sorrows of your existence.

You love us as your own children, with the heart of a father and the heart of a mother, because you are the friends of God.

Listen to our prayer and our request *(state the request)* and intercede for us with God the Father, through Jesus Christ Our Lord, in the grace of the Holy Spirit.

AMEN.

CHAPTER SIX

What Does the Church Say About How and Where I Get Married?

Frequently asked questions

W e've covered an awful lot about marriage in the Catholic Church in this book so far; however, there are often specific questions or concerns that a couple has as they start to plan their wedding. If you have others which are not covered here, talk to your parish priest and he will clarify matters for you.

The references are taken from the 1983 *Code of Canon Law* (*CIC*) and the *Catechism of the Catholic Church* (*CCC*).

My fiancé is a Muslim/Jehovah's Witness/Atheist – can we still get married in the Catholic Church?

Yes. Many couples today marry someone of a different faith. If your future spouse is a non-Catholic Christian, this is referred to as a 'mixed marriage', and permission can be given by your bishop, which you would obtain via your parish priest (*CIC* 1125). If he/she is non-baptised (of another faith such as Islam or perhaps no faith at all), this is known as 'disparity of cult' (*CIC* 1086). A dispensation must be given in this instance, which is likewise obtained from your bishop through your parish priest; you will be able to marry once this is obtained. It is important to bear in mind the material covered in Chapter Five, however, particularly the risks posed to the Catholic party, and any future

PLEASE DO NOT
PARK IN FRONT OF
CHURCH ENTRANCE

A wedding is part of the worship of the Church

children you may have, of lapsing from the practice of the faith. Be sure to discuss the importance of your faith with your fiancé(e), and the promise that you will make to raise your children in the Catholic Church. If they feel similarly strongly about raising your children in their particular faith, then you will need to have a serious discussion about the matter before proceeding further with your wedding plans.

My future spouse is not Catholic – can we have a Nuptial Mass?

Perhaps. Whether or not it is the best option, however, is a matter for discussion between the two of you and your parish priest. A wedding is part of the worship of the Church, and for two Catholics, having it take place in the context of the celebration of the Eucharist is a wonderful start to their marriage. While ordinarily a non-Catholic is not able to receive Holy Communion at a Catholic Mass, there is provision for this in exceptional cases (*CIC* 844.4), and the Catholic Bishops of England and Wales in their document *One Bread, One Body*, have recognised situations where this may be appropriate. This may not be something your non-Catholic spouse wishes to do, however, and in addition to whether or not both bride and groom receive Communion, there are other aspects which you should take into consideration. If many of your guests are non-Catholic, a Nuptial Mass may not be understood or appreciated by many of the people present. If one party is a non-baptised Christian, however, the norms laid down by the many of the Bishops' Conferences exclude the marriage from being celebrated within Mass. It is important to re-emphasise, though, that the rite of celebration of marriage outside of Mass is a full Catholic marriage liturgy.

Are we able to get married in a non-Catholic church?

Perhaps. In order to comply with the law of the Church, a wedding should take place in the parish church (*CIC* 1118.1), and if both parties are Catholic it should present no problem to do so. However, where one of the parties is non-Catholic, a dispensation from canonical form can be given to enable you to marry in another church. There should be a sufficiently good reason, not that you prefer a prettier church for example. Such reasons might include a Church of England bride who wishes to marry in her own parish church, or one of the parties' father may be a Baptist minister whom the couple would like to conduct the wedding. A dispensation to marry in another Christian church may be obtained from the bishop on recommendation of your Catholic parish priest. In this case, the officiating non-Catholic minister is empowered by the bishop's dispensation to receive the couple's consent on behalf of the Church. (*CIC* 1108.2). In addition, Catholic marriage instruction would be carried out by the Catholic parish priest in accordance with the requirements of the diocese. This would ensure that both parties are suitably prepared and aware of the essential properties of marriage (*CIC* 1125.3).

Can we get married on the beach?

No. While *CIC* 1118.2 makes provision for the bishop to permit a wedding to take place in "another suitable place", there must be a grave reason for asking to do so. An example of such a dispensation from Church Law (canonical form) might be at a hospital bedside perhaps, where one of the parties is gravely ill. However, sentimental or aesthetic reasons are not sufficient. It may be a romantic thought to get married where you proposed, or where your family and friends can enjoy a wonderful holiday for less than the price of an English wedding. But it is important to bear in mind that a Catholic marriage is a solemn promise made before God whereupon you ask his blessing. The appropriate place for a marriage to take place is in the house of God.

May we write our own vows?

No. Since a Catholic marriage has essential elements (unity, indissolubility and openness to children) it is important that the couple promise to enter into marriage as the Church understands it. Because of the utmost importance of consent, everyone must be clear that this consent has been declared. If the promises aren't clear, or use wording that may appear to exclude one of these elements, the validity of the marriage may be called into question. Moreover, a Catholic wedding is a liturgical celebration, which is an action involving all of the people of God. It does not belong to us in that respect, and is therefore not open to changes which are of our own personal creation. The bond of communion between the members of the Church is seen in her "common celebration of divine worship, especially of the sacraments" (*CCC* 815) – this unity would be hard to recognise if everyone started altering important parts of the liturgy. Bishop Villegas of the Philippines remarked that personal expressions "should not be mixed in with the Church's liturgy because this diminishes, confuses, and spoils the action of Christ himself in the sacrament." Personal testimonies and declarations of love could be written on the inside cover of the wedding programme perhaps, or form part of a speech at the reception.

I am Catholic and my future spouse is Church of England. Can we have a Church of England wedding with a Catholic blessing?

This is possible. The dispensation from Church Law must be given for you to marry in a Church of England church, and this means that by law the marriage must be conducted by a minister of the Church of England. It is a pastoral practice, however, for the Catholic priest to be invited to give the Nuptial Blessing at the end of the ceremony, as a gesture of support for the couple and a sign of Christian unity between believers of different Christian denominations. Your parish priest should be happy to do this if he is free on that date, and if you so wish.

Are all marriages in the Catholic Church sacramental?

No. Baptism is the gateway to all other sacraments (*CCC* 1213). Other sacraments cannot be received unless a person has first been baptised. However, as with mixed marriages between and a Catholic and a non-Catholic Christian, a dispensation for marriage is usually given by the bishop through his Chancellor or Vicar General upon application from the Catholic parish priest who is instructing you for marriage, and the marriage into which you will enter will be a valid marriage and a permanent union of husband and wife. It brings with it all the rights and responsibilities of a Christian marriage. This is sometimes referred to as a 'natural bond marriage', and is strengthened by the Lord with a sacred seal. Every valid marriage – sacramental or not – is an indissoluble, true marriage.

My fiancé(e) is divorced – are we able to be married in the Catholic Church?

Perhaps. If your fiancé(e)'s first marriage is not considered valid by the Catholic Church, then you can be married in the Church. However, this is a fairly complex matter and your parish priest will need to ask questions to ascertain your particular situation. Basically, no matter your legal status (married, separated or divorced), the Church holds that a valid marriage is indissoluble and therefore would consider your spouse still validly married unless it was declared otherwise. (Canon 1060 states that marriage enjoys the favour of the law – marriages are presumed valid unless shown otherwise.) Some examples where a divorcee may marry in the Church include: if your fiancé(e) is Catholic and was married in a registry office or somewhere other than a Catholic church without a dispensation from canonical form, the marriage may be considered null (this needs to be backed-up with documentation by the Diocesan Tribunal). If he or she has already been through the annulment process and been granted a declaration of nullity, then you would be free to marry in the Church. This question cannot be satisfactorily answered in a few short sentences, since each case is unique and there are many variable factors. I suggest you talk to the Judicial Vicar of the Diocesan Marriage Tribunal, or the Chancellor of the Diocese since this is their area of expertise. You should be able to find their phone numbers online, but if not, your parish priest will provide them for you.

Do I need to be confirmed before I get married?

It's advisable. Canon Law states that "Catholics who have not yet received the sacrament of Confirmation are to receive it before they are admitted to marriage if it can be done without grave inconvenience" (*CIC* 1065.1). If you have the time and are able to prepare for Confirmation before your wedding, it would be a good idea – the gifts of the Spirit received in the sacrament of

Confirmation include wisdom, understanding, counsel, fortitude, knowledge, piety and fear of the Lord, all of which will help you in your married life. However, if the situation is such that you have no time to prepare for Confirmation before your wedding, or if you have reservations about doing so, then you are able to marry without being confirmed. If the issue is a time constraint, you should proceed to complete preparation for the sacrament of Confirmation after your wedding and be confirmed as soon as you are able.

Do we have to complete marriage preparation?

Yes. Canon Law requires that priests offer assistance to the Christian faithful, to include "personal preparation to enter marriage, which disposes the spouses to the holiness and duties of their new state" (*CIC* 1063.2). It is important that the couple have time and opportunity to reflect upon the marriage into which they are about to enter. It is common for parishes to request at least six months in order to have time to complete this preparation, but you can embark on a programme of marriage preparation as soon as you have decided to get married. As mentioned earlier, a lack of full consent, or exchanging promises whilst not intending to actually keep them (for example, having no plans to accept children, or deciding that you will get a divorce if your marriage doesn't work out) can call the validity of your marriage into question. If you and your future spouse do not live near each other, it is possible to take marriage preparation classes separately, although it will require more effort on your part to spend time discussing the different elements of the class.

May we have non-Scripture readings at our wedding?

No. Again, as with writing personal wedding vows, this is because your wedding liturgy is an action of the whole Church and must reflect the solemnity of the occasion. Solemn doesn't mean gloomy, but it does mean dignified and deeply sincere. The Scripture readings included in the wedding liturgy are the Word of God, in whose presence you are getting married and from whom you are seeking blessing. The Word of God speaks to us if we listen. If you have a poem or other piece which is meaningful to you, the wedding reception may be the best place for its recitation.

My father is deceased. Can my uncle walk me down the aisle?

Of course! We discussed earlier that the Catholic preference is for bride and groom to walk in together, signifying their free consent to marriage. However, it is customary for the father to escort his daughter, and if there is a reason why he is not able to do so, any friend or relative can walk you down the aisle. You also have the option of walking down by yourself, if you wish.

Do our bridesmaids and best man have to be Catholic?

No. The witness for the Church is the bishop, priest or deacon, and the other witnesses (of which there must be two) can be anybody you wish provided that they fulfil the age requirement.

Are we able to choose songs which are meaningful to us, but are not hymns?

Probably not. Ecclesiastical music for the bridal procession or recessional music is entirely appropriate, but secular songs such as "Wind Beneath My Wings", for example, are not suitable for a Catholic liturgy. Again, you are marrying before God in God's house. Your wedding is an act of worship and the hymns and music you choose should be in keeping with this.

Should we go to Confession before our wedding?

Yes! It is entirely appropriate, and would be a good idea, for Catholics to go to Confession before receiving a sacrament such as marriage or Confirmation even if we are not aware of committing serious sin. We are better disposed to receive the sacramental grace fruitfully if we are spiritually prepared. If we are aware of serious sin, however, which includes sexual intercourse before marriage, it is necessary to go to Confession before receiving Holy Communion. The sacraments of healing, which include Confession and Anointing of the Sick, have the power to forgive sin and restore us to God's friendship. Do not be afraid of going to Confession – everything you tell the priest is bound by the seal of the confessional and will never be repeated. Nothing you say will shock him; he's heard it all before and will rejoice in your seeking forgiveness and reconciliation with God – that's the reason he's there!

TO DO

● Go to Confession, especially if you haven't been for a long while. The process of conversion cannot begin until we are honest with ourselves. "If we say we have no sin, we deceive ourselves, and the truth is not in us. If we confess our sins, he is faithful and just and will forgive our sins and will cleanse us from all evil." (*1 Jn* 1:8-9)

REFLECT

"The liturgy is not about you and I. It is not where we celebrate our own identity or achievements or exalt or promote our own culture and local religious customs. The liturgy is first and foremost about God and what he has done for us."

Cardinal Robert Sarah

PRAY

There are many times in God's story of salvation that people have not understood what God was asking of them. When the angel appeared to Mary at the Annunciation, she was confused – how could she be having a child when she had no husband? Yet, her obedience to God was complete and unhesitating, and when she visited her cousin Elizabeth shortly thereafter, she offered up the most beautiful words of praise. Today, we call this prayer the Magnificat, or the Canticle of Mary, and we too can pray these words:

And Mary said:
"My soul proclaims the greatness of the Lord
and my spirit rejoices in God my Saviour;
because he has looked upon the humiliation of
    his servant.
Yes, from now onwards all generations will call
    me blessed,
for the almighty has done great things for me.
Holy is his name,
and his faithful love extends age after age to
    those who fear him.
He has used the power of his arm,
he has routed the arrogant of heart.
He has pulled down princes from their thrones
    and raised high the lowly.
He has filled the starving with good things,
    sent the rich away empty.
He has come to the help of Israel his servant,
    mindful of his faithful love
– according to the promise made to our
    ancestors –
of his mercy to Abraham and his descendants
    forever."

(LUKE 1:46-55)

CHAPTER SEVEN

Your Wedding Ceremony

The Rite of Marriage

The Rite of Catholic Marriage is a liturgical act of worship. You may never have thought about it like that before, but a wedding is much more than two people coming together to be married in the presence of family and friends, as joyful and as wonderful as that is. It is an act of worship and thanksgiving of the whole Church; two people being married enriches the Church, and as well as God blessing your union, the whole Church celebrates with you! It is partly for this reason that there are particular norms to the liturgy, consistent elements which focus not just on us, but on God.

Every part of a wedding liturgy, then, gives thanks and glory to God. This should be reflected in the music we choose as well as our attire. The readings are to be chosen from Sacred Scripture, usually from an approved list for weddings, to ensure that they suitably reflect the Word of God which speaks to everybody.

Nuptial Mass or marriage outside of Mass?

Whether you have a Nuptial Mass or a marriage outside of Mass will depend upon the faith of the spouses. If you are both Catholics, it would be fitting for the two of you to get married during Mass. The Eucharistic celebration – the re-presentation of Christ's sacrifice on Calvary, the act from which our redemption and all grace flows – is the "source and summit of the Christian life" (*CCC* 1324). To exchange wedding promises and enter into married life in the context of the Mass, and to receive Holy Communion as your very first act as a married couple is a very powerful thing.

If one of you is a non-Catholic Christian, however, it is worth giving the matter some thought and discussing it with your priest. In receiving the Eucharist in Holy Communion we are saying that we are 'one in communion', firmly holding and professing all the Church teaches, and so the Church usually does not give Holy Communion to those outside the Catholic Church (with the exception of Eastern Rite – or Orthodox – Catholics). As mentioned in the previous chapter, there is a provision in the document *One Bread, One Body* (which bases its guidance on the *Code of Canon Law*) for non-Catholics to receive Holy Communion not only at times of "grave and pressing need", but also on a "unique occasion for joy". The non-Catholic party may wish to receive Communion, in which case have a word with your priest, but if they do not wish to receive Communion, the Rite of Marriage outside of Mass would be the better decision.

If one of you is not baptised, then the Rite of Marriage should take place as a separate liturgical service; in this instance the reception of Holy Communion would not be possible by the non-Catholic spouse. It is important to restate that a wedding liturgy is full and complete, whether it takes place inside or outside the context of Holy Mass.

A Nuptial Mass or wedding liturgy is an act of worship

Readings

The readings should be appropriate for a wedding liturgy. They are a proclamation of God's word and reflect Church teachings about marriage. Your priest should have a booklet you can borrow which lists some of the most suitable readings – take some time to read them through and see which you would like. A wedding service will usually have a reading from the Old Testament, a Psalm, a reading from the New Testament, and a Gospel reading. For a list of approved readings, see Appendix Three.

Music

Music for a wedding must be suitably dignified to reflect the solemnity of the occasion. This does not mean that the music has to be sombre, but it does mean that it should not be trivial or secular in nature. The music at a wedding should reflect the beauty and the dignity of a liturgical service, since it heralds a couple who are coming before God to be joined in a nuptial union. Orchestral and organ pieces should be classically beautiful, and while hymns are appropriate, secular songs are not. This is fundamentally because, as mentioned before, a Nuptial Mass or wedding liturgy is an act of worship which involves the whole Church. Hymns are appropriate because they are songs of worship and praise offered to God. There are many uplifting hymns which reflect the joyful nature of a wedding – you may have some favourites in mind, but if not, the organist will have some suggestions. Some suggestions suitable for a wedding in England are included in Appendix Four, although different countries and cultures will have hymns which reflect their traditions.

A short anecdote: a good friend of mine who is an organist told me about a couple who came to him to choose their wedding music. The bride wanted to come down the aisle to the tune of *Daisy, Daisy, Give me Your Answer, Do.* Yes, her name was indeed Daisy, and the lyrics were not completely inappropriate per se, but I don't think anyone would argue that this song is a dignified piece! Perhaps it would be better suited to the reception, after which they could leave on a bicycle built for two...

Choir

If you would like a choir at your wedding, to 'augment' the singing shall we say, since guests are often reluctant to sing with gusto, it is worth asking the organist if there is a choir which sings at the church where you will be married, and whether they are happy to sing at your wedding (sometimes the choir may only sing at Sunday Mass). If there is no choir, the organist may know of other options.

Altar servers

If you are having a Nuptial Mass, it may be nice to have altar servers present. The altar server assists the priest; as well as performing small tasks, a server can bring a polished look to the Mass. If you have a server, you will be able to have bells at the consecration and if you have two or three, you will be able to have incense too. So think about what you would like for your Nuptial Mass and talk to your priest, who will know if there are any servers who are willing to serve at a wedding.

Offertory procession

Again, with a Nuptial Mass, the bread and wine will need to be brought forward to the altar in an offertory procession, although it is not required if nobody is able to do it. This usually involves two or three people carrying the gifts from the back of the church to the priest and altar servers, if any. You will need to choose someone happy to do this – this can be a role for family, such as grandparents or younger cousins, to help those without a major 'role' to feel included.

Ushers

Ushers add a nice touch to your wedding, although they are by no means necessary. Their usual role is to greet guests, hand them their order of service and show them to their seats. In the UK, it is traditional that the bride's guests sit on the left of the church and the groom's on the right, although more recently people are often encouraged to sit where they wish. It's nice for the church to have a balanced look, and the usher can keep an eye on that, encouraging, for instance, that mutual friends of the bride and groom sit on the emptier side of the church (often that of the member of the bridal party with the smaller family). The ushers can contribute to the dignity of the wedding by ensuring that latecomers are escorted discreetly to their seats and that any unforeseen events are handled with the minimum of fuss. The role of usher can also include things from making sure everyone present can get to the reception (some guests may need to beg a lift), to acting as an escort with an umbrella in the case of rain, and other thoughtful touches which take into consideration the comfort of the guests.

Wedding attire

Wedding attire is a big deal, with dresses and cravats and bridesmaids dresses and mother of the bride hats being topics of conversation of the utmost importance for months beforehand! It is a very special day, and everyone wants to look their best. The attire should bear in mind, though, the common thread running through this whole chapter which is that a Catholic wedding liturgy is a solemn ceremony taking place in the house of God.

I will touch on modesty because it is linked to beauty. Tight revealing dresses can make a woman look sexy, but that's not the same as beautiful, and I don't think it's prudish to think the latter is preferable to the former for a wedding ceremony. Fashions come and go and sleeves happen to be currently making a bit of a comeback. Remember that fashion designers are playing to the market, and a lot of brides will be marrying in a registry office or a different venue, such as a country house hotel. Even of those marrying in Church, many will not be aware of their marriage as a sacred liturgy. With all that we have covered, it should be clear that something transcendent is taking place and wedding attire should reflect this dignity.

The bridal veil is also a very special part of the bridal attire. Veils throughout Judeo-Christian history have been used to signify something holy, or set apart. Tabernacles in Catholic churches are often veiled because they contain the sacred, life-giving presence of Christ in the Eucharist. Women have been set apart for their beauty and cherished for their ability to nurture new life. A veiled bride symbolises the mystery of marriage, and unveiling the bride is a very lovely tradition. I want to emphasise that the Church does not intend to act as the fashion police, but these things are presented for your consideration in the light of understanding your wedding as a sacred liturgy, and the place of appropriate dress in the house of God.

Flowers

Flowers are a matter of personal preference and will be influenced by your budget, since they can be quite expensive. As well as bridal and bridesmaids bouquets, a larger arrangement is often made for display in front of the altar. Smaller arrangements can be attached to pew ends. The florist you choose may be familiar with your particular church and have some ideas. The flowers in the sanctuary (in front of the altar, on a pedestal perhaps) are usually left for the weekend Masses. You can take the pew ends and other flowers with you and use them as floral table pieces at the reception.

Customs and traditions

Different nationalities and cultures have different customs which form part of the wedding ceremony. Some couples place a special bouquet at the statue of Mary in the church, as a sign of devotion to Our Lady. Other cultures place a large rosary around the shoulders of both bride and groom, signifying a binding together by God; this is popular in Filipino, Spanish and Latin American ceremonies. The unity candle – a recent tradition which is gaining popularity in the USA – is a candle lit by the couple to signify two becoming one. The bride and groom bring their own taper candles and together light the larger unity candle. This tradition is not part of the liturgy and will be done towards the end, before the final blessing perhaps.

If you have a particular custom which is meaningful to you, mention it to your priest and see what he has to say. He may very well be happy to incorporate it into your wedding ceremony.

Stipends

While there is no charge for a wedding in the Catholic Church (unlike the Church of England, which has a fixed fee for weddings), it is customary to give the priest and other key members of the wedding ceremony a monetary gesture of thanks. This is known as a stipend. If you are well off, you may want to give more than a couple who barely has two pennies to rub together. Since there is no set fee, people are reluctant to pick a figure, which can be annoying if you're not sure how much to give. Asking around, I came up with the following averages: priest (or deacon) – £120-£160; organist – £50-£75; altar server – £20. Somebody else mentioned that the stipend for the priest should be about the same amount you spend on the wedding cake. If you have a choir at your wedding, they will usually have a set fee and let you know what that is when you book them.

Confetti anyone?

Definitely check with your parish priest on confetti! Some churches will not allow it because of the mess it makes, while others do not mind. Other churches allow guests to throw rice since this is much less visible and will be eaten by the birds. The tradition of scattering rose petals is sometimes allowed, since they are biodegradable, but then again, other churches say they are a slipping hazard and will allow a few silk rose petals if they are swept up afterwards. Each parish will have their own set of ideas about what they will and will not permit, so don't forget to ask.

One last thing

A wedding does not have to be lavish to be beautiful. It does not have to cost a fortune, with thousands of pounds spent on flowers and a dress to rival the bride in a royal wedding! There are many ways to keep the budget within your means, by choosing seasonal flowers instead of exotic blooms for example, and by keeping the arrangements simple. A lot of stress within any marriage can come from money worries, and to go into marriage with a lot of unnecessary debt is not the best way to start.

TO DO

- *Make a separate wedding checklist for your wedding liturgy. An example is found in Appendix Two.*

REFLECT

But in order that the liturgy may be able to produce its full effects, it is necessary that the faithful come to it with proper dispositions, that their minds should be attuned to their voices, and that they should co-operate with divine grace lest they receive it in vain. Pastors of souls must therefore realise that, when the liturgy is celebrated, something more is required than the mere observation of the laws governing valid and licit celebration; it is their duty also to ensure that the faithful take part fully aware of what they are doing, actively engaged in the rite, and enriched by its effects.

Second Vatican Council, *Sacrosanctum Concilium*

PRAY

Prayer of a future husband

Blessed are you, O God of our ancestors, and blessed too is your name forever. Let the heavens bless you for evermore and all the things you have made. It was you who created Adam, you who created Eve his wife to be his help and support; and from these two the human race was born. It was you who said, "It is not good for the man to be alone; let us make him a partner like himself."

I take N in sincerity of heart. Have mercy on her and on me and allow us to live together to a happy old age.

(ADAPTED FROM TOBIT 8:5-7)

Prayer of a future wife

Keep me, O God, for in you I take refuge; I say to the Lord, "My God are you. Apart from you I have no good." I bless the Lord who counsels me; even in the night my heart exhorts me. I set the Lord ever before me; with him at my right hand I shall not be disturbed. Therefore my heart is glad and my soul rejoices, my body abides in confidence.

You, O Lord, will show me the path to life, fullness of joys in your presence, the delights at your right hand forever.

(ADAPTED FROM PSALM 16)

CHAPTER EIGHT

Your Married Life

A period of adjustment

Going from being an unmarried couple to 'Mr and Mrs' requires a period of adjustment. Husband and wife have different characters and personality traits and will be negotiating how best to manage a shared life. This is an ongoing process, since circumstances change over the years requiring readjustment to the new circumstances. These can be joyful events, such as the birth of a child, or a promotion and house move, but even joyful events are often stressful and stress can bring out the worst in people.

This process of adjustment will present itself even if a couple has been living together before the wedding, since there is a fundamental spiritual and psychological change in their relationship. This can manifest itself in different ways, from feelings of disappointment and anti-climax that things don't feel different enough, to feeling trapped or claustrophobic because there's a new level of commitment. For all couples, no matter how well they know each other, things are different now – there is no walking away when things get tough. Hence the first year of marriage can be – for many people – a significantly stressful time.

Conversely, you may enjoy an extended honeymoon period and transition smoothly into married life, but in all these cases, it is important to be realistic in your expectations. You found a person you want to share your life with, but sometimes you will get on each other's nerves. This is normal. There is no such thing as a 'soul mate' or a lifetime of 'happily ever after' – at least not in the way Hollywood portrays it. Many people think they've made a mistake in choosing who they thought was 'the one' only to find out after leaving the relationship and entering into successive relationships that there really is no such thing. Of course, there are people we simply could not live with because they drive us round the bend; chances are, though, that we would have left a relationship like that long before we start planning the wedding!

Difficulties can be weathered as long as expectations are realistic and the commitment remains strong; these difficulties do not mean that a relationship is doomed. It's important we try not to get discouraged.

Called to love

You're getting ready to promise 'to love and to cherish', but the word love is freely used and its meaning is not always clear. Other languages have different words for love – ancient Greek has six – each denoting a different type of love (brotherly love, erotic love and so on). Unfortunately, English has only one, and one which can be applied to everything from spousal love to the love of ice cream. Clearly, the meanings are very different. Now, promising 'to love' implies that love is a verb and not just a feeling. You cannot promise to control your feelings, only your behaviour, and this is very important to remember. There will very likely be times when you don't feel very much in love, but that is no reason to think you have made a mistake.

As we said in Chapter One, love is desiring the genuine good of the other. That sounds quite simple, and in theory it is, but not so much in practice. To see the perfect example of love, one need only look at the crucifix – God so

loved the world that he gave his only Son so that whoever believes in him shall never perish but have eternal life (*Jn* 3:16). Jesus restored us to life – and at what cost! There will be times that we have to make sacrifices and we will often rail against it. But the crying baby needs food and we will awaken at 3am to feed him or her. It requires we keep going, even when we don't feel like it, but the rewards it brings are worth the sacrifice.

Spousal love requires that we support each other, perform acts of service and generally work together for the good of each other and the good of the family. But someone's genuine ultimate good is to reach heaven, and we should desire that for them. Any action which puts that in jeopardy is not an act of love.

Establishing priorities

We live in a finite world. We have a limited amount of hours in the day, and days in the year. Similarly, we have a pot of money which is not bottomless. We can't do everything we want – even if we only had ourselves to think of, there would still be decisions to make. Factor in our spouse who may have different priorities to ours, and we have the potential for conflict.

Ask anyone the most common areas in which couples disagree and you will probably come up with money and child raising. Money is definitely a big one – one spouse may be a careful saver, while the other spends money more freely. Even if we both agree on spending the money (instead of saving it) we have to decide whether to go on holiday or get a better car. Both are legitimate options, and each spouse may think their idea is the better one.

How we spend our time is important – how much time should we spend with your mother? Shall we go out or stay in? As a couple, or with friends? So many decisions...

Broad directional goals may also differ – do I place a very high priority on a good career? Do I consider my work at the service of providing for my family, or does my family take a back seat to career progression?

Some of these issues can become matters over which a couple can dig in their heels. Arguments can lead to resentments, and the marital relationship can really begin to suffer. Since there are often no right or wrong answers, the key to establishing priorities can be summed up in a few short words: effective communication, consideration of the other person's wishes and desires, and willingness to compromise.

Communication is the key

Communication is the key to solving problems. Of course, even effective communication can fall on deaf ears if one spouse is hard headed about their opinions, but remember you are a couple now. You're a team. The competition should not be between the two of you. Love requires sacrifice and compromise, and if you both take the time to listen with care and express your viewpoint calmly, you are in a good starting place.

Communication, to be effective, must be respectful. Screaming and name calling are also forms of communication, but not especially constructive ones; the same applies to sarcasm and cruel comments. There are many articles and books which aim to guide us through the seemingly complex business of communication, and this may be something you wish to look into further. But a good rule of thumb is to state our thoughts clearly and avoid accusations so that our spouse is not put on the defensive, since a defensive person is hardly likely to be eager to accept our point of view. Respect ensures that a comment remains a statement of our feelings and desires and not a personal dig or judgement of your spouse's character. Speaking is only part of the communication, however; listening to what the other says is also very important. We must really hear them and absorb what they are saying, while avoiding the temptation to formulate our own response before they've even finished making their point.

Married life is beautiful, and must be protected

Respect one another

Stereotypes do not always hold up and can sometimes be a dangerous place to venture, however while men and women need to feel both loved and respected, women generally have a stronger need to feel loved and men a stronger need to feel respected. This plays out in fairy tales – the princess wants to be loved and swept off her feet by her handsome prince, who in turn wants to be the brave hero. Since people often give affection and affirmation in the way they would like to receive it, showing love generally comes more easily to women and showing respect tends to come more easily to men.

This knowledge can be key to a more harmonious relationship. If a husband feels respected, he will willingly move heaven and earth for his wife, and if a wife feels loved, she too will go above and beyond to make her husband feel appreciated. Perhaps it was because of these inclinations that St Paul wrote in his letter to the Ephesians that women should respect their husbands and husbands should love their wives – the exhortation is for each to do what generally doesn't come easily.

Mutual respect goes a long way to help ensure that we give the benefit of the doubt to our spouse. Instead of assuming that someone does not care for us if they forget our birthday or otherwise 'mess up', we assume goodwill. Assuming motives that may not be true starts to subtly move us towards condemnation of the other person, placing on our relationship a filter through which we view the actions of our spouse. We should make a point of always trying to assume our spouse's *good* intentions, and when tempted otherwise, to make a conscious effort to maintain mutual respect.

Forgive one another

Even if we have a respectful relationship and assume the goodwill of the other, there will still be times when our spouse hurts us and we hurt them. In loving another, we become vulnerable; by allowing another access to our heart, we give them the ability to wound us, and if they do something which hurts us deeply, we can feel greatly betrayed. This is readily apparent in cases of infidelity, which can cause tremendous harm to a relationship, but resentments can also build over things such as being late home from work without calling, for not doing something you said you'd do (such as taking the rubbish out), or saying hurtful things in the heat of the moment during an argument.

There are two options from which to choose when people hurt us. We can hold on to the negative feelings, bear the grudge, and allow the bitterness to embed itself in our heart, or we can forgive. The bitterness which can take hold in a marriage where grudges are held and scores kept can poison a marriage over time. It turns the time we spend together into a negative experience, and can snuff out the mutual affection which should be shared between spouses.

Christians don't have the option to refuse forgiveness, however – it is commanded of us repeatedly in the Scriptures. We must forgive not seven times, but seventy times seven (*Mt* 18:22). The Lord's Prayer asks God to "forgive us our trespasses as we forgive those who trespass against us"; if we wish mercy to be shown to us, how can we withhold it from others?

If someone does hurt us badly, and perhaps repeatedly, then we must forgive them but we do have a right to protect our heart by establishing boundaries. If our spouse is clearly in the wrong (and this judgement must be made with due care since it's always easy to blame the other), it is not in their best interest for us to indulge them. We are not called to become doormats or enablers. These situations can often be complex and may require a couple to seek help from a friend, priest or counsellor.

When the honeymoon is over

I'm not sure if there are any couples who have a life-long honeymoon. Maybe there are. But for most of us, life is busy and demanding and reality very quickly kicks in. The endearing quirks of our spouse now manifest themselves as annoying habits. The expectations we had about those Sunday afternoon relaxing strolls may be replaced with a huge pile of laundry which needs to be done ready for the new working week. This is completely normal and requires both an acceptance of the situation as well as a focused and determined effort to make time to nurture our spousal relationships.

Sometimes, however, a marriage can hit a real crisis. At times like this it can be very tempting to call it a day and we completely forget the "for better, for worse" part of our wedding promises. Some situations – such as domestic violence – may very well require a separation for the safety of spouse and children. These situations don't account for most divorces, however – far from it. Many people separate because the shine has worn off, they can't speak without bickering, and they simply do not 'feel in love' any more. At times like this, it is incredibly difficult to remember our covenant relationship, but a marriage is sacred and anything worth having is worth fighting for. There are marriage enrichment weekends which can help strengthen communication and there are programmes like *Retrouvaille* which help couples experiencing marital crises.

You may have heard the phrase 'work like everything depends upon you and pray like it all depends upon God'. This is true in marriage too – never underestimate the power of grace. We should go to Confession regularly – being forced to confront our own sin shines the spotlight on us and encourages us to see our contribution to any particular situation. The strengthening power of the Holy Eucharist and the grace obtained through prayer, while an important part of our everyday life, can give us extra strength when times are hard.

Lastly, even the pope is under no illusions that marriage is a walk in the park! He spoke about marriage towards the beginning of his pontificate, recognising that stress can manifest itself in outbursts of emotion:

The plan inherent in marriage is truly wonderful! It is expressed in the simplicity, and also in the fragility, of the human condition. We are well aware of the many difficulties and trials there may be in the life of a married couple....

It is true that married life has many difficulties: work, there isn't enough money, there are problems with the children...and often the husband and wife become irritable and argue amongst themselves. There are always arguments in marriages, and at times even plates are thrown. But we must not be sad about this: this is the human condition. And the secret is that love is stronger than the moments in which we argue, and I therefore always advise married couples never to let the day draw to an end without making peace. There is no need to call in the United Nations peacekeepers. A little gesture is enough: a caress, see you tomorrow, and tomorrow we start afresh. This is life, and we must face it in this way, with the courage of living it together. Married life is beautiful, and must be protected.

Pope Francis, Catechesis on the Sacrament of Marriage, 2nd April 2014

TO DO

● *Think a little about the way you communicate as a couple. Is it respectful and kind? Be conscious of the things you say and how they may be perceived by your fiancé(e), in other words, take some time to step back and see if you like your style of communication. If it needs adjusting, now's the time.*

REFLECT

Marriage is also an everyday task, I could say a craftsman's task, a goldsmith's work, because the husband has the duty of making the wife more of a woman and the wife has the duty of making the husband more of a man. Growing also in humanity, as man and woman. And this you do together. This is called growing together. This does not come out of thin air! The Lord blesses it but it comes from your hands, from your attitudes, from your way of loving each other. To make us grow! Always act so that the other may grow.

Pope Francis

PRAY

The Memorare is a prayer to Our Lady which can be used when things seem difficult or discouraging. Add it to your repertoire of Catholic prayers – it is well to remember that Our Lady cares about your trials and will intercede before her son for you and your marriage.

Remember, O most gracious Virgin Mary,
that never was it known that anyone who fled
to thy protection, implored thy help, or sought
thine intercession was left unaided. Inspired
by this confidence, I fly unto thee, O Virgin of
virgins, my mother; to thee do I come, before
thee I stand, sinful and sorrowful. O Mother
of the Word Incarnate, despise not my petitions,
but in thy mercy hear and answer me.

AMEN.

Conclusion

Marriage is a truly good institution, blessed by God, recognised by society, and deeply appreciated by our families and communities. From strong marriages come strong families, and from strong families comes a strong society. Marriage is a time honoured tradition which has been around for aeons, and so it's easy to take it for granted and not think too deeply about it. But times are changing: years ago, people usually married for life, but these days, a lot of people marry more than once, while some choose not to marry at all.

What is needed is a renewed understanding and appreciation of the institution of marriage. We need to revisit its meaning in order for us to see that it is not something we do just for the two of us because we think it will be fun. Marriage is the foundation upon which society is built, and has been for generations. It provides a stable environment for children to grow and thrive, being formed into tomorrow's men and women of honest character and integrity. Like the Church's teaching on sexuality, a better understanding of marriage can take us from how it *feels* to what it *means*.

In order to live according to our God-given human nature, we are called to love. Made by God who is love, we are drawn to communion with him, both in this life and in its fullness in eternity, and as we journey in this life, we are also drawn to communion with others. It is in giving love and friendship that we find fulfilment, and in doing so we receive love and friendship back. More than friendship, however, we all seek that particular and special 'someone' with whom we are closely bound, in a relationship which resembles friendship but which transcends it. The complete union of husband and wife in marriage is unique among human relationships, and possesses a particularly noble dignity based on its potential to create new life with God.

So, yes marriage is a coming together of hearts and minds. On your wedding day, you will join together as one and start out on a new leg of your life's journey, together this time. The mutual affection you feel for one another

and the interests you share are to be celebrated. The natural attraction you feel for each other will grow into deep bonds of trust and intimacy as love matures. As you embark on your life as a married couple, be sure to cherish your marriage, treat it with care as you would something of great value, for that is what it is. Nurture your love and make it a priority to spend time together so that you don't drift apart.

There will be times, however, when daily life can be difficult. Different stressors can take their toll on our mood, and we often take this out on those closest to us. The thought that we may have made a mistake may pass — hopefully only fleetingly — through our minds. At times like this, we need to remember our wedding day and our promises, and what it was about our spouse that made us sure we wanted to marry them. In periods of difficulty, as well as good times, recourse to prayer and the sacraments keeps us strong in our marriage, and gives us the grace to overcome whatever particular trials we may be going through at the time.

My hope is that the information and opportunities for reflection found in these pages will give the reader pause for thought about marriage. Aware of the dignity of marriage and its covenantal status, we can better appreciate the beauty of the indissoluble one flesh union. By considering the family as an icon of the Holy Trinity in its total and fruitful love, we can more perfectly

Love is always ready to trust, to hope and endure

appreciate the blessing of children, seeing them as a gift and never a burden. Mindful of the real and powerful nature of sacramental grace, we can see that marriage is a divine reality, and one which strengthens the whole Church. The reflection exercises and questions can help us understand ourselves and each other better, and ensure that we are aware of the expectations we both bring to our marriage.

It is often easy to forget that Jesus is found in the small acts of kindness of our life. Indeed, he is found in the not-so-pleasant mundane routine of our day. All we do, we should strive to do for love of others and for love of God. In this way, we live our vocation to marriage in a manner which is both pleasing to God, and pleasing to our spouse and family.

The following words of St Paul are timeless. They may well be quite familiar, since they are a very popular choice for a wedding reading, but due to their familiarity, we often don't give them the focused attention they deserve. Spend some time with them now and read them carefully:

Love is always patient and kind; love is never jealous; love is not boastful or conceited, it is never rude and never seeks its own advantage, it does not take offence or store up grievances. Love does not rejoice at wrongdoing, but finds its joy in the truth. It is always ready to make allowances, to trust, to hope and to endure whatever comes.

Love never comes to an end. But if there are prophecies, they will be done away with; if tongues, they will fall silent; and if knowledge, it will be done away with. For we know only imperfectly, and we prophesy imperfectly; but once perfection comes, all imperfect things will be done away with. When I was a child, I used to talk like a child, and see things as a child does, and think like a child; but now that I have become an adult, I have finished with all childish ways. Now we see only reflections in a mirror, mere riddles, but then we shall be seeing face to face. Now I can know only imperfectly; but then I shall know just as fully as I am myself known.

As it is, these remain: faith, hope and love, the three of them; and the greatest of them is love.

(1 Co 13:4-13)

St Paul reminds us that love is always ready to trust, to hope and endure whatever comes; we do not understand God's plan in the complexities of this life, and we do not know what the future holds, but we believe that we will see clearly in the end. Faith, hope and love – known as the theological virtues because they dispose us to live in a relationship with God – are the foundation of a Christian life (*CCC* 1813). Faith is a belief in things not seen, and hope is the desire we have for heaven, trusting in the promises of Christ. Love is the greatest because it is the measure by which we will be judged. In eternity, faith and hope are no longer required because we shall see "face to face".

Love however will always remain, because God is Love.

Appendix One

─── ♌ ───

Family of Origin Reflection Questionnaire

In marriage, two individual people with different character traits and from different family backgrounds are joined together. Our early formative years and family experiences will have helped shape who we are, and it is important to be aware of what may underlie your assumptions or expectations.

The following questions are points for reflection which will help identify similarities and differences in your experiences and opinions. By discussing them, it will help avoid the disagreements and even conflict which may later arise.

Answer the questions individually, and then compare your responses. This exercise is designed to help facilitate communication; if there are any important areas in which you strongly disagree, you may wish to seek the advice of a person you trust.

Your parents' marriage

Have a think about your parents' marriage. Your *perception* of their relationship will have influenced your understanding of marriage growing up, even if this does not reflect their lived reality.

Roles and attitudes

- Who was responsible for childcare and housework?

- Did your parents have an equal relationship in terms of maturity, or did one parent 'mother' or 'father' the other?

- Did your parents love and support each other, or did they berate and belittle each other?

- Was either parent manipulative or controlling?

- Did either of your parents suffer from addiction or mental illness? If so, how did you cope with that and are those coping strategies helpful or destructive to your current relationships?

Expressions of love and affection

- How did your parents express their love for each other? Were they physically and verbally demonstrative, or reserved and private?

- Did they help and support each other in practical ways?

- Were they faithful to each other?

Conflict and problem solving

- How did your parents resolve conflicts? Did they discuss matters respectfully, or were they verbally abusive?

- Did they have loud arguments, or instead resort to the silent treatment?

- Did you see a willingness to apologise to each other?

Decision making

- How did your parents make decisions? By discussion and consensus, or by one assuming the authority to act?

- Did your parents work together as a team when discussing plans for the family?

- Who decided where to go on holiday, about home improvements or similar projects?

- If there was a 'one-sidedness' to the decision making, was this willingly agreed to or met with resentment?

If your parents divorced

- Are you worried about your ability to form a lasting marriage?

- Do you feel that it isn't possible for a couple to stay together forever?

- Do you worry that your future spouse may walk out on you?

Reflecting upon these questions will help you think about whether you have adopted these behaviours in your own relationship. If you have done so, was it intentional? If it was unintentional, do you need to make a concerted effort to modify your behaviour or expectations? Are there areas which you assumed you would bring to your marriage, but in which your future spouse isn't so keen? Use this information to facilitate some respectful discussion. It will help you to better understand your future husband or wife, and be more aware of your attitudes and behaviours.

Appendix Two

---ᶜᵍ---

Wedding Liturgy Checklist

6-12 months before:

- Make appointment with priest
- Book wedding date/time (in fact, do this as soon as you've decided to get married! This could be 18 months in advance)
- Discuss wedding liturgy
- Registrar required?
- Arrange marriage preparation classes

3-4 months before:

- Obtain wedding license
- Choose readings
- Approach reader(s)
- Arrange meeting with organist
- Choose wedding music and hymns
- Arrange printing of Order of Service
- Make appointment with florist to arrange flower arrangement
- Choose ushers
- Ask church 'policy' regarding confetti
- Ask priest about any restrictions on photography/videography
- Check with photographer to ensure he is familiar with your church venue

If you are having a Nuptial Mass:

- Enquire about altar servers
- Arrange for two or three guests to bring forward offertory gifts

2 -3 weeks before:

- Touch base with your priest to make sure everything is in place
- Wedding rehearsal booked?
- Stipends – place each in a marked envelope and arrange for an usher to hand them out directly after the ceremony.

Appendix Three

Suitable Readings for Your Wedding

Source: *www.liturgyoffice.org.uk/Resources/Marriage/OCM-Lectionary.pdf*

Old Testament readings

Gn 1:26-28, 31a – Male and female he created them.

Gn 2:18-24 – They become one body.

Gn 24:48-51, 58-67 – Isaac loved Rebekah, and so he was consoled for the loss of his mother.

Tb 7:6-14 – The Lord of heaven favours you, my child, and grants you his grace and peace.

Tb 8:4b-8 – Bring us to old age together.

Pr 31:10-13, 19-20, 30-31 – The woman who fears the Lord is the one to praise.

Sg 2:8-10, 14, 16a; 8:6-7a – Love is as strong as death.

Si 26:1-4, 16-21 – Like the sun rising is the beauty of a good wife in a well-kept house.

Jr 31:31-32a, 33-34a – I will make a new covenant with the House of Israel and the House of Judah.

Responsorial psalms

Ps 32 (33):12 and 18, 20-21, 22. R. 5b – The Lord fills the earth with his love.

Ps 33 (34):2-3, 4-5, 6-7, 8-9. R. 2a or 9a – I will bless the Lord at all times. Or: Taste and see that the Lord is good.

Ps 102 (103):1-2, 8 and 13, 17-18a. R. 8a or cf. 17 – The Lord is compassion and love. Or: The love of the Lord is everlasting upon those who hold him in fear.

Ps 111 (112):1-2, 3-4, 5-7a, 7bc-8, 9. R. cf. 1 – Happy the man who takes delight in the Lord's commands. Or: Alleluia!

Ps 127 (128):1-2, 3, 4-5ac and 6a. R. cf. 1 or 4 – O blessed are those who fear the Lord! Or: Indeed thus shall be blessed the man who fears the Lord.

Ps 144 (145):8-9, 10 and 15, 17-18. R. 9a – How good is the Lord to all.

Ps 148:1-2, 3-4, 9-10, 11-13ab, 13c-14a. R. 13a – Praise the name of the Lord. Or: Alleluia!

New Testament readings

Rm 8:31b-35, 37-39 — Nothing can come between us and the love of Christ.

Rm 12:1-2, 9-18 (long form) or 1-2, 9-13 (short form) — Offering your living bodies as a holy sacrifice, truly pleasing to God.

Rm 15:1b-3a, 5-7, 13 — Treat each other as Christ.

1 Co 6:13c-15a, 17-20 — Your body is the temple of the Holy Spirit.

1 Co 12:31-13:8a — If I am without love, it will do me no good whatever.

Ep 4:1-6 — One Body and one Spirit.

Ep 5:2a, 21-33 (long form) or 5:2a, 25-32 (short form) — This mystery has many implications and I am saying it applies to Christ and the Church.

Ph 4:4-9 — The God of peace will be with you.

Col 3:12-17 — Over all these to keep them together and complete them, put on love.

Heb 13:1-4a, 5-6b — Marriage is to be honoured by all.

1 P 3:1-9 — You should all agree among yourselves and be sympathetic; love the brothers.

1 Jn 3:18-24 — Our love is to be something real and active.

1 Jn 4:7-12 — God is love.

Rv 19:1, 5-9a — Happy are those who are invited to the wedding feast of the Lamb.

Gospel readings

Mt 5:1-12a — Rejoice and be glad, for your reward will be great in heaven.

Mt 5:13-16 — You are the light of the world.

Mt 7:21, 24-29 (long form) or 7:21, 24-25 (short form) — He built his house on rock.

Mt 19:3-6 — What God has united, man must not divide.

Mt 22:35-40 — This is the greatest and the first commandment. The second resembles it.

Mk 10:6-9 — They are no longer two, but one body.

Jn 2:1-11 — This was the first of the signs given by Jesus — at Cana in Galilee.

Jn 15:9-12 — Remain in my love.

Jn 15:12-16 — What I command you is to love one another.

Jn 17:20-26 (long form) or 17:20-23 (short form) — May they be completely one.

Appendix Four

Suitable Music for Your Wedding

Music for your wedding should be dignified. When choosing your hymns, ask yourselves:

- Is it beautiful?

- Do the words worship God?

- Are the words suited to a wedding liturgy?

- Is it well known, so that your guests will probably be familiar with it?

If you are having a Nuptial Mass, you might also consider singing some parts of the Mass.

Some suggestions: (NB these may be appropriate for an English wedding. Other countries will likely have different customs and cultural traditions which extend to hymns and wedding music.)

Entrance of the bride

- Arrival of the Queen of Sheba

- Trumpet Voluntary

- Grand March from Aida

- Bridal Chorus

- Canon in D

Hymns

- Love Divine all Loves Excelling

- Lead Us Heavenly Father Lead Us

- Lord of all Hopefulness

- Praise My Soul the King of Heaven

- O Perfect Love

- Praise to the Lord, the Almighty the King of Creation

- All People who on Earth do Dwell
- O Worship the King
- How Great Thou Art
- Oh God Beyond all Praising (Thaxsted)
- All Creatures of Our God and King

For the signing of the register or presentation of flowers to Our Lady

- Ave Maria (Schubert or Bach/Gounod)
- Jesu, Joy of Man's Desiring
- For the Beauty of the Earth (Rutter)

Exit of bride and groom

- Wedding March (Mendelssohn)
- Trumpet Voluntary
- Hornpipe (Handel)
- The Rejoicing (Handel)

PICTURE CREDITS: